Land of the Sun Kings

DRAWN FROM PERUVIAN RUINS, from the neglected archives of Spanish conquerors, and from exciting new archaeological discoveries, this is the detailed, engrossing history of the ancient Inca empire, the fabulous land of the Sun Kings, which once stretched over two thousand miles along the South American coast.

Here a veteran explorer traces the growth of a mighty realm from a primitive settlement in an Andean valley to a vast nation linking more than two million people in a complex welfare state. He tells how the Incas united their subjects with a common language and matched the engineering feats of the Romans with lofty bridges and royal roads. Their brilliant creative achievements are revealed in fascinating descriptions of their art, huge agricultural projects, and imposing temples. In these pages, too, are the contrasting lives of the people—the harsh, spartan existence of the peasants and the dazzling luxury of the Lord-Inca, with his harem, glittering gold-plated palaces, and sumptuous robes discarded after a single wearing. And the author vividly recounts the kingdom's sudden downfall, when a small band of Spanish conquerors extorted from the terrorized populace a treasure-room of gold worth $200,-000,000.

Complete with over 50 drawings, maps, and photographs, this fascinating book reveals the genius of a brilliant dynasty which, unaided by the art of writing or even knowledge of the wheel, became the richest and largest of the Pre-Columbian civilizations.

A distinguished American explorer of ancient Western Hemisphere cultures, Victor W. von Hagen has written over a dozen books about Latin America's past and the men who have uncovered it.

Other Books by VICTOR W. von HAGEN

EXPLORATION:

Off With Their Heads (1937)
Ecuador the Unknown (1938)
Jungle in the Clouds (1940)
Ecuador and the Galápagos Islands: A History (1949)
Highway of the Sun (1955)

BIOGRAPHY:

South America Called Them (La. Condamine, Humboldt, Darwin, Spruce) (1945)
Maya Explorer, The Life of John Lloyd Stephens (1947)
Frederick Catherwood: Architect (1950)
The Four Seasons of Manuela (1952)

ARCHAEOLOGY-ANTHROPOLOGY

The Tsatchela Indians of Western Ecuador (1939)
The Jicaque Indians of Honduras (1943)
The Maya and Aztec Papermakers (1943)
The Aztec: Man and Tribe (1958; MP364)
World of the Maya (1960; MP394)

Realm of the INCAS

Victor Wolfgang von Hagen

Illustrated by Alberto Beltrán

Revised Edition

MENTOR: ANCIENT CIVILIZATIONS
Published by THE NEW AMERICAN LIBRARY

MENTOR BOOKS are published by
The New American Library of World Literature, Inc.
501 Madison Avenue, New York 22, New York

Contents

Part Four   The Achievements

List of Illustrations

Figures

vii

Plates

(*between pages 112-113*)

Part One

THE HISTORICAL AND GEOGRAPHICAL BACKGROUND

1 How We Know What We Know About the Incas

THE INCAS arrived late.

This is a fact—it might have been otherwise—yet it has long been known and accepted that man in South America had fashioned many amazing civilizations before the advent of the Incas.

There are thousands of books and pamphlets about the Incas. Merely to collect them all you would have to have much of the golden loot that was to ransom Atahúalpa, for many of the best books about the Incas are scarce and expensive; further, only to thumb through all the published material that deals with them in one form or another, involving oneself in the disputes over trivia, is alone a life study.

The whole history, from the beginning, will be both paradox and puzzle. Since the question will spring up within the very first pages it might as well now be asked and answered. All of the prehistory of the South Americans is shadowy: not one of their cultures had writing; we do not even know with absolute certainty the name of any of these people, and not even the name of the people of the Incas (for that term was applied only to its rulers). The knot-string records—the famous *quipus*—have no key without the aid of the professional "rememberers" who could read them; now to us they are only lifeless strings. There are here no "talking stones" such as appeared among the Mayas, no folded books with rebus writing as the Aztecs had; there was no kind of writing of any form, no matter how much some scholars may strain their imaginations. There is not even a single absolute time element one can seize upon. The only certain

11

date is 1527, for in that year Francisco Pizarro touched for the first time the shores of the realm of the Incas.

How then, if all this is true, does the archaeological historian speak so knowingly about the Incas? From what sources all the detail that follows? How can an archaeologist, like a theologian who talks of eternity, speak so knowingly of the unknowable?

Somewhat this way.

The records started immediately with the Spanish conquest in 1532. An "Anonymous Conqueror"[5] first wrote down in vivid homespun prose the matter-of-fact details of this fantastic conquest of a fantastic kingdom; of how millions of Indians were brought to heel within an hour by 130 foot soldiers, and this, published in 1534 only a few months after the event (even containing a crude woodcut of the Lord-Inca himself being borne aloft by his litter-bearers), began the literature.

Next came the reports made by the soldier-secretaries of *the* conquistador; these are earthy and informative, couched more in the style meant for the daily business of human lives than with the lyricism one expects to herald the death throes of a barbaric kingdom. It is true, these reports lack details, their concepts of geography are vague, yet they convey a good picture of the Inca peoples, their land, roads, buildings, and there are wonderfully descriptive pictures of the golden ransom sent by the empire to free their Lord-Inca held captive by the small band of Spaniards. One of these, Pedro Pizarro (who actually participated in the conquest), wrote down his memories—larded, however, with highly sententious fantasy.[49]

Then there are other reports which in effect begin the literary avalanche on the "Inca," for following the unadorned soldierly reports came those scribes who spent the night scribbling their reports. They were attached to the officials whose job it was to root out the riches of the Incas. They are full of contumely. But in 1547 a simple soldier named Pedro de Cieza de León ("simple" here synonymous with "intelligent") turned up in Peru.[14] He came riding down the full length of the Inca highway from Colombia. At last one is on solid ground. A man of infinitely good sense, he has provided much that is in this book. His first book, published in 1553, went through six editions in as many years. Soldiers, scribes, and lawyers cribbed from him. Then come the narratives from the new race—the Cholos, half-Inca, half-Spanish. There are a goodly number of them. The best-known writer is, of course, Garcilaso de la Vega, son of a knight and a royal Indian lady, who wrote his *The Royal Commen-*

taries of the Incas in Spain.[21] Another, not so well known, is Felipe Guamán Poma de Ayala, who wrote and illustrated *The First New Chronicle and Good Government*[50]—it is difficult to read but valuable since it is profusely illustrated with pen drawings; it is a primary source for the dress and customs of the Incas. Yet no one in Peru or Spain ever heard of the author, the book was never printed until 1927,

1. *Self-portrait of the Inca-Spanish chronicler Felipe Guamán Poma de Ayala in Spanish attire of the sixteenth century, seen talking to Indians, from whom he gathered the basic material and drawings for his book* The First New Chronicle and Good Government *written between the years 1560-99. It was lost until found in the Royal Library at Copenhagen in 1908.*

and when it was found in the beginning of the twentieth century it turned up, of all places, in the Royal Library at Copenhagen.

The seventeenth and eighteenth centuries ushered in the epoch of the priest-chronicler; and even though the material on the Incas is manipulated to fit into an existing Christian pattern, much of the details on dress, customs, religion, food, government are excellent. Of these histories, that by Bernabé Cobo is "the best and most complete description of Inca culture in existence." [53]

The eighteenth century brought in the period of enlightenment and with it began the scientific explorations to Peru, and from out of these came many detailed observations, culminating with the works of the great Alexander von Humboldt,[29] who gave us the first truly accurate descriptions of Inca roads and buildings. It is with these that the modern era of archaeology begins.

After William Prescott had written the *History of the Conquest of Peru*,[52] long-lost or forgotten manuscripts came to light and were published; three more of Pedro de Cieza de León's wonderful Inca histories were found, and hundreds of other reports were brought to light under the impulse of renewed interest in the *Conquest*.[40] And they still are. Sir Clements Markham followed Prescott and himself appeared in Peru (Prescott never did), and although Markham himself penned no epics, he did fan the fire of Inca enthusiasm by translating numerous old Spanish chronicles which have been the fount and source of scholars for a century.

The Peruvians themselves began now to take an interest in their own past, so much so that when E. George Squier appeared in Peru in 1863 as Abraham Lincoln's representative, Peru was already conscious of its past greatness. One of the first "dirt" archaeologists, Squier began the physical examination of the "evidence"; his book, *Peru: Incidents of Travel and Exploration in the Land of the Incas* [62] (1877) marks the beginning of this modern approach, and still can be read with pleasure and profit. The next writer of real consequence to appear is a German. For forty years Peru and other countries occupied by the Incas were examined by Max Uhle. He collected widely and well from funds sent to him by Mrs. Phoebe Hearst of California, the result being that those selfsame archaeological pieces have nurtured in California three generations of archaeologists. Many of the most prominent ones cut their archaeological teeth on Max Uhle's collections.

If one examines the literature one can see how the wand of the archaeological relay is handed from one to another. In 1911 Hiram Bingham, a young American historian, appeared in Peru. He was actually looking for Vilcapampa, the last capital of the Incas, when he accidentally discovered the fabulous stone city of Machu Picchu. That discovery gave the new generations as much impulse toward Peruvian archaeology as Prescott's writings had given the past. With Bingham was another young historian, Philip Ainsworth Means. He remained behind and over a period of years wrote a series of books that nicely mingled scholarship and archaeology. His *Ancient Civilizations of the Andes* (1931) and the *Fall of the Inca Empire and the Spanish Rule in Peru, 1530–1780* (1932) will remain source books for all time.

The last twenty-five years have been the years of systematic excavation and stratigraphical archaeology. Peruvians, notably the late Dr. Julio C. Tello, following the scent of oral history, dug up cultures such as Paracas and Chavín and many others, which had never been in the archaeological lexicon. Regrettably, Tello wrote little, but he was in his way (even though much criticized by his fellow archaeologists as having been a sort of Giovanni Belzoni, who broke into the pyramids with a battering ram, trampling on golden-plated mummies as "thick as leaves in Vallambrosa") an archaeological pathfinder and has opened myriads of new avenues into the roads of the past. Peruvians, a few French, Germans, and many Americans have published widely and thoroughly on far-ranging aspects of Inca and pre-Inca cultures. In 1931, the Shippee-Johnson Aerial Expedition to Peru discovered many unknown sites from the air. Since that time aerial exploration has given a new dimension to Peruvian archaeology and the aerial mosaic is now standard equipment for the investigator. With new techniques, principally the carbon-14 tests—a method of dating through the measurement of the rate of disintegration of radioactive carbon in active matter—and with controlled stratigraphical surveys of ancient sites, the archaeologists have in some instances "fixed" the dates of some of these ancient civilizations.

All that was known up to 1945 of the material culture of the Incas, along with other South American cultures, was published in the encyclopedic-sized *Handbook of South American Indians*,[63] written by the world's leading authorities on the subject. For the nonspecialized reader it will perhaps tell him more about South American Indians than he wants to know, yet it is all there—and in full measure.

So the hero of this, if there is one, is the archaeologist, he who has sat in the dust of history and patiently pushed back the layers of detritus, in a way like turning the leaves of a book, out of which he has read the past.

2 The Geographical Background of a Culture

IT WAS Bartolomé Ruiz, the first Spanish navigator to sail the windlashed Peruvian seas, who provided those others who followed him with sailing instructions. When asked how in all this incomprehensible desert land they could know when they had made the correct landfall to the "Kingdom of Gold," he replied: "When you no longer see any trees, you are in Peru." It was not wholly true, of course; still it was good enough to serve a navigator for laying down a course to Tumbes, the first port of call of the Spanish conquest.

Tumbes, or Tumpiz as it was then pronounced, was in fact the last northern coastal city of the realm of the Incas. North of this frontier city there is a sharp topographical line, and the humid tropics, a luxuriant jungle begins and continues northward to Panama. South of Tumbes, or rather at Tumbes, the brazen desert begins and extends, except when broken by occasional valleys, for two thousand miles southward.

The forces of nature in this extremely confined coastal desert (it varies between one to twenty-five miles in depth between the sea and the Andes) have always been of supreme importance; here, as in few other places in the world, climate was (and still is) the vital factor that shaped human lives.

First, the strange sea, the cause of it all. It rushes onto the coast in huge unhurrying rollers roaring in from the turbulent coastal current without. The phenomenon of a cold current in a tropic sea has had marked effect on the land, for here normally rain never falls and the entire length of this coast is reduced to an extreme waterless desolation. The mountains loom up out of the desert like dry bones; the whole aspect of it in its entire length is hollow and fainting: "A place where," said one of the first Spaniards, "there is no water, no trees, no grass nor any created thing except birds which by the gift of wings wander wherever they will." [14]

For more than half of the year the heat of the sun is of such force as to broil one's brains, but between May and November the skies, due to a further cooling of the cold current, cause heavy mists to pour over the littoral, and the days are overcast and grim. A haze overhangs the land during the day, and at night it dulls the glamor of the stars.

Plankton is carried on the bourn of this ubiquitous current, the passively floating animal-plant life, so minute as hardly to be seen by the naked eye but in so incalculable a multitude that it pigments the ocean stream. This life is avidly fed on by the sea fauna, rich and varied, which in turn attracts the sea birds (in such astronomical numbers as to darken the skies). These birds, to complete this interlocked life cycle, nest on off-shore islets where they deposit their guano dung, the most concentrated nitrogen-rich fertilizer known in the world.

Although along this 2000-mile-long desert coast there are more than forty valleys, between each lies the lifeless void of desert. Rivers, large and perennial, others small and occasional, which have created these valley oases cut through the towering Andes and rapidly descend into V-shaped valleys bringing every year a renewal of fertile silt.

Early South American men filtered into these valleys and formed into tribes; in time they extended these valleys by careful irrigation, increasing artificially and unnaturally the areas of fertility. And so, as each tribe was isolated by desert from the other, they developed over great reaches of time highly individual traits and cultures.

Since trees were rare here in ancient times, the idols of these coastal dwellers were of wood; since mud and sand were the base of their material culture, they built of sun-dried brick, and their most fabulous cities were in reality only plastic mud. Since here the sun was always menacing and was *not* to be appeased, they selected as their principal deity the moon, which controlled the sea.

So Man here became the catalyst of the desert.

Yet one of the most remarkable civilizations did not originate in this environment. The *Incas* instead were one day to emerge as a tribe and empire in the Andes. They appeared in a high, treeless tableland, a region of long grass, a land which is seared by the noonday heat and made frigid by night. This was the land of the *Keshwas* (or Quechuas), the "warm-valley people"; their name in time was to be given to the language of the Incas.

There is not one Peru but three, and all these three Perus lie parallel to each other: coastal deserts, high mountains, and low-lying jungles. It is these three discordant geographies which the Incas were to coalesce into empire.

The temperate zone in the Andes lies in the grass areas at a land height above 9,000 feet; it is a region that is capable of sustaining an intensive agriculture. Here in this purlieu, trees were also rare but there was rock, so stone became the source of these Andean peoples' culture. As the sun's appearance was limited and the making of sun-dried adobe hampered building with it, stone became the primary building material, and the fabulous cities of these mountain tribes were put together with intricate stonemasonry. Since the life-giving sun was life-warming, it became their principal deity.

Man here became the catalyst of the Andes and bent this rock-hard world to his will.

The imposing Cordilleras in Peru's center march southward in a double array of mountains as in two chains; they spread apart into a vast oval at 14°3″ south latitude, and this becomes the basin of Lake Titicaca. Still farther southwest and down into Argentina and Chile the Andean chains break into a tangled mass of mountains and salt marshes, and eventually emerge into immense rolling pampas which are also treeless. On these plains primitive man, intensely wild and untamed, hunted the ostrich and wild guanaco.

The deep valleys of the Cordilleras (as the first Spaniards called the mountains) take the run-off of the water and form it into numerous rivers, which emerge into the gigantic rivers Huallaga and Ucayali, both tributaries of the Amazon. This is the jungle, the third of the three Perus.

Actually the forest begins as montaña at 6,000 feet altitude, for it is ceaselessly wetted from the rain-bearing trade winds which collide with the Andean spurs that slant sharply east. The Montaña is heavily matted with vegetation. It has lofty cloud jungles, deep valleys covered with forest, and wildly plunging rivers; this is the *yungas*, a Quechua word applied both to the hotlands and to the people living there.

The eastern slopes of the mountains are inexorably flattened until they become finally a vast carpeted forest broken only by rivers which flow through the green mansions of trees, propelled by the eastern slant of the land into the Amazon. Here to plant one tree you must first cut down twenty. In this terrifying luxuriance a totally different people lived—fierce, independent, cityless warriors who were armed with poison-tipped darts which curdled the blood when stuck in flesh. They too were farmers, jungle farmers, but they resisted any form of organization and so only the margins of the jungle yielded to the soldiers of the Inca.

These, then, are the three Perus, and out of these three contrasting geographies—desert, mountain, and jungle—the Incas hammered out, *à la repoussé* their fabulous realm. No matter what form of society that lived in this ancient Peru—whether it was the effete Chimú, who surrounded

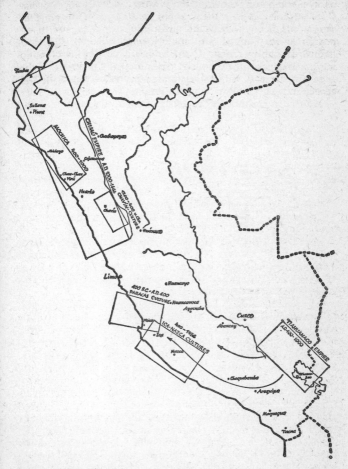

2. *Distribution of pre-Inca coastal and Andean cultures. The range is between 1200 B.C. and A.D. 1466. The Tiahuanacan culture, although here centrally located, is assumed to have originated about Lake Titicaca. These people made a complete conquest of the coast* (A.D. 1000-1300).

himself on the desert coast with gold and ease, or the head-hunters in the jungle, who made out of their slain enemy's head a mimicry (tsantsa) the size of a fist, all were brought into the orbit of the Incas.

All phenomena, it seems, felt the Inca influence: the

people, the plants, the animals, the very names over the land.

The whole Andean area, as Philip Ainsworth Means once wrote ". . . is colored indelibly with the Inca dye. And to this day, in every part of the territory once ruled by the Incas [from Colombia through to Argentina, from the desert coast to the jungles] one is hourly conscious of the ghost of the Incas' supremacy manifesting itself in scores of ways: through speech, customs and material culture."

All this, even though the Incas arrived very late.

The Pre-Inca Cultures: Chavín
3 — Mochica — Paracas — Nazca — Tiahuanaco — Chimú

EVERYTHING, or almost everything, in Peru, as is evident, had antecedence over the Incas. Archaeologists have peeled back the layers of Peruvian prehistory until their spades have come to rest on sterile cultural earth, and they know that the story that archaeology tells us in Peru is this: a succession of cultures endured for millennia, and in many instances died out, before the Incas arrived to engulf the whole land and to organize its conquest-acquired inheritance into an empire.

That we have almost no history of many of these pre-Inca cultures other than that which archaeology reveals, we owe principally to the Incas themselves, for in their conquests they snuffed out the others by their own "selective manipulation of remembered history." [46]

For not only were the earth and the peoples organized by the triumphant Incas but memory as well, and the theme of the Inca as the "civilizer" became their dominant theme. Their thesis was that before their arrival all of South America was a cultural void. This official history was forced upon all those conquered. Memory of past peoples and cultures was systematically purged and subjected to a "sort of editing and selective distortion not entirely unlike the tendentious distortion to which the Spanish themselves subjected it [the Inca history] in their turn." [46] An "official" Inca history was created, local oral traditions of the tribes whom they had conquered supplanted and allowed to lapse. The official "rememberers," who were the Incas' historians, no longer bridged the gap between legendary man and those innumerable pre-Inca cultures, so that this "selective manipulation of history" which was to represent the Incas as being alone the culture bearers, emerged as *the* history of preliterate Peru. All the rest of the pre-Inca histories were allowed to be lost in oblivion.

What then, and who, were all these civilizations, now with-

3. *Chavín. The dominant design of this culture* (1200-400 B.C.) *is the Cat God.*

out name and barely with legend, that preceded the Inca? Who were these people who pioneered in that triumph over life that forced nature, that exigent mistress, to yield plants where there had been none before, who were these who sent water into a waterless land and created domestic animals out of a wild fauna, animals needed for the new burgeoning societies of American man? Space does not permit us, nor is it the object of this book, to detail all of those cultures which preceded the Inca; that alone would be a book. To say everything is to say nothing; to show everything is to make one see nothing. The thing is to light up what is pertinent, and an archaeological excursus, admittedly limited, will I believe show readily enough that which has already been put forward: that for two thousand years prior to the Incas there was in Peru a long steady cultural growth.

As regards precise time, no one can be absolutely sure in Peru of anything in this regard. There was no written literature or history except the litany of "remembered" historical events that was orally passed down through the ages. There were no dated coins, as there were among the Romans, where a Caesar had image and date stamped thereon; the Incas had no money. There is only the one date (1527) which we know with absolute certainty.

And yet with painstaking persistence archaeologists have made progress in unraveling, in the broad, the space-time divisions of these pre-Inca cultures. Archaeological stratigraphy has rolled back the layers of history. The designs on ceramics, which are among the best aids for time analysis (see Pottery and Pottery Makers, page 85), have been carefully studied, and archaeologists have set up for themselves a table of such "horizon styles"; excavation and reconstruction of material cultures, a re-examination of Inca oral traditions, in this new light, have yielded a broad cultural time sequence. The deductions from these are obviously only the bare outlines of history which wait to be detailed with further facts; yet from all this, the late Dr. Wendell Bennett (accepted by his colleagues as the best in this field) conceived the *six periods of South American archaeological history,* admittedly tentative.[8]

The curtain rises (at approximately 1200 B.C.), with Period I. Man has already been on the north desert coast of Peru for a long time. He has had pottery and weaving since 1500 B.C. He builds structures. He is already growing maize (no doubt with bird guano as fertilizer), and he raises the tuber called manioc. But he is not the first here; there were others long before him, for the remains of their weaving and agriculture, as proven by the carbon-14 tests, show them here as early as 3000 B.C.

The first culture of prominence in Period I is *Chavín;* its leitmotif is a ferocious-looking Cat God found on pottery and stonework and in weavings. This motif was to haunt the cosmology of the ancient Peruvians for the next thousand years.[20] Chavín's center (presumably it was a mecca even during late Inca times) is the site of Chavín de Huantar, which lies in a narrow valley in the Andes beyond the Cordillera Blanca. Here are the remains of impressive buildings characterized by well-laid stone walls and ornamented with stone-carved human and animal heads set in the wall.

Period II, which, it is deduced, fell between the centuries 400 B.C. and A.D. 400, is called, with some exercise of the imagination, the "Experimenter" period because of the supposed experimenting in weaving and pottery by many widely scattered cultures.

Paracas, which lay below Central Peru to the south of Lima near Pisco, is a pre-Inca culture of Period II. It is famed for its textiles, believed to be the finest ever loomed. This culture is wrapped in mystery; we do not know its tribal name nor anything more positive about it than the evidence in their caverns found in the brazen desert and close upon the sea on the Paracas Peninsula. In deep subterranean rooms four hundred or more mummy bundles were found: the flexed bodies were adorned with superbly woven shawls, turbans, and robes, all in the most exquisite polychrome embroidery. Little is known about them beyond these remains. They, and

4. *Nazca pottery. Finely made, it is characterized by use of abstract decoration. Its motif: the Cat God holding severed heads.*

the culture which preceded them by five hundred to a thousand years (and which used the same area for their burials), made use of the natural desert sands for mummification. The Paracas appear in no remembered annals and are unmentioned by the Incas.

By the time of Period III, between A.D. 400 and 1000, man has completely dominated his environments of the desert coast and the Andes. He has acquired wit and cities. It is the period of high craftsmanship in architecture, ceramics, and weaving. On the coast the *Mochicas* (we have no idea what they called themselves) are a caste-minded empire; they lord it over the northern Peruvian desert and one can still see the remains of their temples, one of which, called Huaca del Sol, in the Moche Valley is constructed of approximately 130,000,000 sun-dried adobe bricks. This suggests, naturally, a complex social organization to accomplish so effective a construction; the advancement of their society is given further emphasis by their skill in gold casting and wood carving. Their weaving is thought to have been done on a shop basis, for on one Mochica vase a man, obviously a chieftain, sits under a frilled sunshade and directs rows of women busily engaged in weaving on their back-strap looms. The Mochicas had warriors, messengers, weavers, and "doctors"; they built roads and organized a courier system, and perfected many a

5. *Paracas culture (400 B.C.-A.D. 400) is easily defined by its superb weavings. This is the complete costume of a man from the acropolis of Paracas Peninsula.*

social pattern that appeared later in the political organization of the Inca.

In a verdant valley, Nazca, south of Paracas, which breaks the naked misery of the desert, is another lost culture, lost to history because its own history was purposely "dismembered" by the Incas—the *Ica-Nazca*. This cultural area is now somewhat less of a mystery and is being unraveled by the archaeologists. Fine weaving and excellent ceramics were emphasized, and not too distant in design from those of Paracas. Architecture, however, is not a dominant feature, and little remains to tell us how they lived. Like the others,

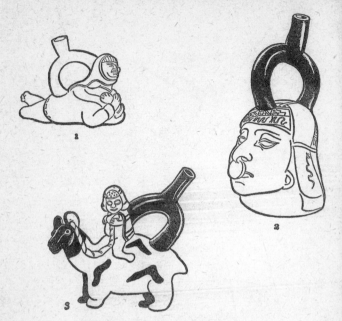

6. *Mochica pottery, coastal culture* (A.D. 400-800). 1) *Historical evidence of the successful amputation of legs as shown in the realistic representations of warriors who underwent operations. Drawn from the costal pottery of the Mochicas* A.D. 400-800. 2) *The pottery of this period is so realistic it might be considered as portraiture.* 3) *Man riding a llama. Drawn from Mochica pottery circa* A.D. 800. *A costal llama with a rope through its ear is guided by a man with an amputated foot.*

they are anonymous. The greatest mystery of the Ica-Nazca cultures is the vast network of "lines," a fantastic assembly of rectangles and squares that have been etched into the sand and waste gravel. Outsized birds, spiders, whales, and sur-realistic figures are also present. These lines, some running for miles in length, have remained in a good state of pres-ervation, showing this land to have been, then as now, a desert of everlasting drought. These lines are approximately fifteen hundred years old. They could be calendary ob-servations or they could be genealogical symbol "trees." What is now positive, at least, is one date: an American archaeolo-gist found a wooden "sighting" stump at the end of one of the lines and carbon-14 tests have placed it close to the date of A.D. 500.

It is known that sometime close to A.D. 900 a mountain

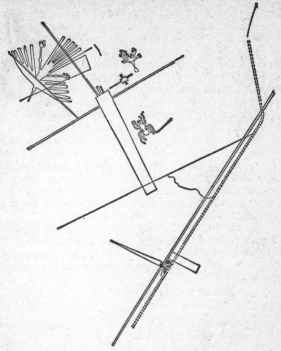

7. *The mysterious lines and figures in the valleys of Nazca. These first begin to appear in the Pisco valley. They are mostly concentrated in the five valleys of the Nazca. This drawing, made from an aerial photograph with ground reconnaissance, shows some of the rectangular lines and the realistic and surrealistic figures. The heavy-lined road is the ancient Inca highway, built circa A.D. 1400; the dotted lines are the modern Pan-American Highway. Drawn by Pablo Carrera from the notes and photographs of the author.*

people called the *Tiahuanaco Empire* came to the coast in a religio-military invasion, sweeping down from their stronghold centered about Lake Titicaca. They had then an interest in astrology, a solar calendar, and, as well, a sort of shadow clock. It is highly possible that the Tiahuanaco culture brought the technique of the "lines" to Nazca before their cult of the Weeping God.

Whatever the origins of all this, the Incas allowed nothing about them to come down to us. For the "lines" of Nazca, they had full contempt; those practical Inca engineers ran their 24-foot-wide coastal road directly through them.

The empire of Tiahuanaco is the dominant civilization of Period IV (A.D. 1000–1300) in Peru and Bolivia. Like all the other pre-Inca cultures, it has left us only unexplained mysteries. The remains of what must have been the greatest ceremonial center in all the Andes are still to be seen on the Altiplano in Bolivia, near Lake Titicaca at an altitude of 12,500 feet. Dr. Wendell Bennett thought "Tiahuanaco the most elaborate and the purest manifestation of the culture yet to be found up to this time."

The stonework of Tiahuanaco developed centuries before the Inca work, and until their advent, it was the best in the Andes. Stones are fitted together with insets and tenons; larger stones are bound with copper clamps. All this architectural megalithic stonework presupposes a social organization, a strong central government which could divert the use of manpower into non-food-producing channels of so large a scale. All this must have been done by a large supply of workers with a long technical tradition.

And yet nothing is precisely known of these people or their empire. They too, like the others, are nameless.

That this great culture, Tiahuanaco, should have no oral history points more than any other evidence to the success of

8. *Man receiving a blow on the head. Drawn from a Mochica vase, dated circa A.D. 800. Blows such as this resulted in head fractures, which were often cured by skull trepanning.*

the Incas (who were, in some stage of their development, doubtless contemporaneous with them) in deliberately obliterating all memory of them. For when Pedro de Cieza de León made inquiries in 1549 about the people who built the ruins at Tiahuanaco, the oldest of the Indians then living could not even recall a single fact, and to these inquiries they replied that it had been built long before the Incas ruled but that they were unable to say who had built it.

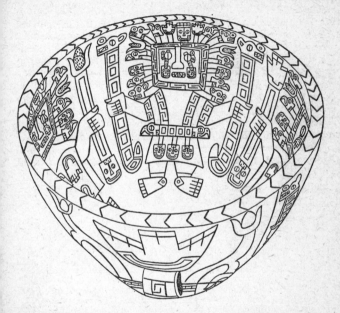

9. *The Weeping God of Tiahuanaco. A large urn, found in Nazca, dating from the Tiahuanaco coastal occupation* (A.D. 1000-1300).

Yet the Tiahuanaca cultural conquest penetrated many of the remote corners of Peru. Many of the contemporary cultures, even the early Inca, adopted the symbol of the Sun God. This Weeping God wept all manners of tears—zoömorphic tears—condor-head tears and snake-head tears. These and other design motifs, such as the puma, trident, and step designs, are widespread along most of the thousand-mile coast. But that conquest, motivated by religious fervor, was not systematically organized, for the Tiahuanaco left behind them little social impress—only those unmistakable designs on pottery and cloth, and the cult of the Weeping God.

The *Chimú Empire* (A.D. 1000–1466), called the Kingdom of Chimor, also belongs to this period even though it extends beyond it into that of the Incas.

The Chimús were coastal people, workers in plastic mud and worshipers of the moon. Their capital, Chan-Chan (which is close where the Spanish-Peruvian city of Trujillo now stands), was eight miles square, replete with enormous step pyramids, rows of houses, great walled compounds, irrigated gardens, and gigantic stone-lined reservoirs.

10. *The Chimú culture, centered about the Virú and Chicama valleys, existed between A.D. 1000 and 1466. The Chimús were workers in plastic mud, and the walls of their capital, Chan-Chan, were covered with designs such as these. Drawn from photographs of the author.*

From Chan-Chan, the Chimús ruled over six hundred miles of coast from Rimac (now Lima), up to the humid tropics of Ecuador. Indirectly, they ruled over much more territory. Everything here was on a large scale: weaving was on a mass basis; pottery, mostly black ware, was produced in molds; whistling jars and cooking pots were mass-produced. Their weavers made superb feather tunics and gold-working was also on a large scale, for the amount of gold yielded to their conquerors, the Incas, was staggering and even that which the Spaniards found much later (which was a mere nothing) reached into the millions. The Chimús developed the roads, taken over from their predecessors, the Mochicas; they developed further the courier communication system, and they extended their political alliances beyond the coastal desert far up into the Andes in order to protect their water supply.

The Chimú Empire was the last of the larger cultures to offer opposition to the Incas. That we know a good deal about the Chimú culture is due only to the fact that before the Inca methods of historical selectivity could be brought into full effect to eliminate the Chimús from human memory, the Spaniards arrived.

The listing of these pre-Inca cultures will seem, as it indeed is, foreshortened; there were many others, but only those of the greatest cultural influence in Peru have been

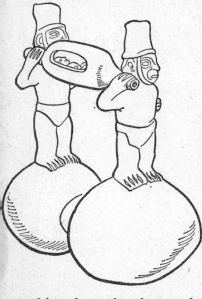

11. *Coastal Indians carrying a child in a litter. Drawn from a Mochica vase circa* A.D. 800.

named in order to show how steady was the cultural evolution that had been going on for three thousand years in Peru before the advent of the Inca.

Many of these civilizations were of the highest level, and from them the Incas drew heavily in order to form the material culture of their own empire. In a sense, and the analogy has often been made, the Incas were like the Romans—inheritors of a vast skein of cultures which became, in the weaving, a complicated tapestry of human progress.

Thus archaeology stands in direct opposition to the form of history which the Incas told of themselves, which is that all of the Andean (and coastal) peoples were savages until the Incas came upon the scene. This special twisting of events by the Inca history-makers is something that bears an ironic resemblance to the living history of the Russians as described in George Orwell's book *1984*.

The story that archaeology does reveal—if one will have the patience first to locate and then go through the infinite number of articles, monographs, and books on this fascinating subject—is this: there was a long succession of cultures before the Inca, and the Incas arrived late and were the organizers rather than creators of Peruvian civilization.

However, as this book will reveal, they were incomparable organizers.

"Inca History Has Its Origin
4 in Myth and Continues in
Legend" [46]

WE KNOW, curiously enough, no more about the origins of the Incas than that which they tell us of themselves in their "remembered" history and mythology. This "official" history embodies a vague legendary memory, but what part is myth, what part history, what mere dialectic, we do not know. And, moreover, there is as yet no precise answer from archaeology. The "remembered" history has it that they came out of, or about, Lake Titicaca, wandered north between the double array of the Andes, came to the valley of Cuzco and there laid the beginnings of empire. That the Incas and their empire *did* evolve within the valley of Cuzco has been at least confirmed by archaeology.

What do the myths say? The Sun God created the first Inca, Manco Capac, and his sister, on the Isle of the Sun in Lake Titicaca.

The Sun God instructed them to set out and teach the arts of civilization to all the other Indians then living in barbarism. Thus begins the apostolic succession of the Incas from the creator-god. Manco Capac carries a golden staff; he has been instructed by the Sun God that when he reaches a place so fertile that the staff will sink out of sight when thrown into the ground, there he is to build his city. The brother and sister set out northward, encountering, as mythical characters do, the usual difficulties, until they arrive at the Cuzco Valley. Manco is moved by what he sees, he throws the golden staff, it sinks out of sight—and Cuzco is born. There are variations on this theme: there are four brothers surnamed "Ayar" (wild quinoa grain), and there are four sisters called "mama," and they live in caves some twenty miles southeast of Cuzco. They set out, find the fertile Cuzco Valley, and then three of the brothers metamorphose themselves into stones or shrines, allowing Manco, with his sisters as his harem, to found Cuzco and begin with them the tribe and the empire. This is the sort of folklore

33

that most peoples invent about themselves. If the mythos of Christianity were reduced to a five-line synopsis, it would have much of this naïveté.

Doubtless the Inca legends are the personification of a small tribe (one of the many which were then living about the fertile regions of Lake Titicaca) who in search of new lands fought their way northward until they came to the valley of Cuzco; there they defeated the original possessors of this Andean glebe. The precise time of Inca emergence is not known. At this time the entire Andean region was broken up into "an almost unbelievable number of small political units," [53] all of different speech, all with different myth patterns. At this time these divers tribes were on about the same cultural level; i.e., they had the same plants under cultivation, they tilled land with the same techniques, and all had the domesticated llama. So the story that the Incas tell of themselves, that they were especially chosen by the Sun God to raise the other Indians from their subhuman ways, to bring arts and culture to those other Indian tribes, *has found no support in archaeology*.

The people called the Incas began—and this is precisely what makes their history fascinating—with the same cultural weapons as all other Indians then living in the Andean regions.

"In the year 1000 A.D.," wrote Pedro de Cieza de León (whom we will meet often in these pages), ". . . in the name of *Tici Viracocha* and of the Sun and the rest of his gods, Manco Capac founded the new City.

"The origins and beginnings of Cuzco was a small house of stone roofed with straw which Manco Capac and his wives built and which they named 'Curi-cancha,' meaning 'Golden Enclosure.' "

This, Pedro de Cieza de León had from the "rememberers" of history in Cuzco in the year 1549; it is as good and simple a historical premise as any.

The Incas stress that they developed within the Cuzco Valley, and the excavations of Dr. John Rowe have confirmed this. "Enough has been done . . . to show that the Inca civilization *was* the product of a long development in the valley of Cuzco itself and that consequently it is unnecessary to look farther afield for that civilization's cultural origins." [53]

It is important that this tangible evidence of archaeology be stressed, to balance, as it were, the present-day insistence that the Incas originated elsewhere; for since the sixteenth century the Incas have been variously described as descendants of the tribes of Israel, the sons of Kublai Khan, Armenians, Egyptians, Chinese and—even Englishmen. Sir Walter Raleigh had it from someone that Manco Capac, the first Inca, was actually a corruption of Ingasman (i.e., Englishman) Copac, "the Bloody Englishman."

The latest spectacular attempt to prove that Polynesia was peopled by Tici Viracocha, the creator-god, this by an expedition on the floating balsa raft *Kon-Tiki*, also has no support from archaeology, nor, still more important, from botany. The Peruvian civilization was built up of *intensified* pre-existing American Indian cultures and not by anything additional or foreign. The Incas developed within the valley of Cuzco and the whole cycle of their mythology contains not even the slightest suggestion of any tribal migrations outside of the Andean region.

They occupied the valley, liquidated the earlier possessors (although just *whom* they replaced is not clear in the archaeological sequences), and they began their polygamous society. They had, it is only repeated for emphasis, the same cultural tools as all other Andean folks: the polished stone celt, forms of agriculture following the same irrigational techniques, the domesticated llama (it had been domesticated for two thousand years *before* the coming of the Incas). And finally they had as the base of their society the earth-cell commune, the *ayllu,* or communally held land.

All this was Andean in pattern. And yet they had something more. They had an innate sense of organization. War

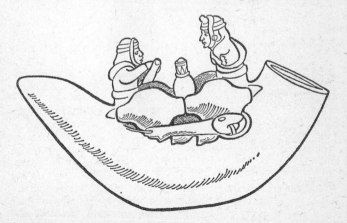

12. *Coastal Indians fishing from a reed balsa craft made from the tubular* totora *grass. In such craft, designed for two or three people, Indians fished at sea. Drawn from a Mochica vase (circa* A.D. *800).*

was no longer an elaborate façade to overawe an enemy; war was to be won and conquest was to be organized. The particular genius which was Inca came out of Cuzco, that small hollow of land and valley, that very Cuzco which is the longest continuously inhabited city in the Americas.

The Incas expanded; they expanded as all empires do—by conquest.

Centuries passed like the moving arm of a weaver's shuttles. The people of the Incas, call them Quechuas, for Quechua was their language, became a disciplined people living

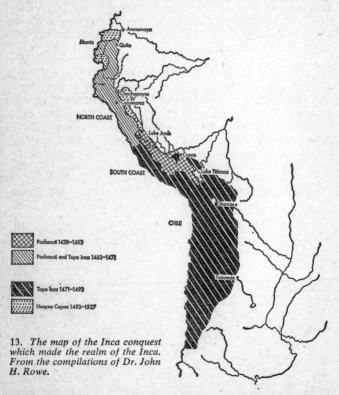

Pachacuti 1438–1463

Pachacuti and Topa Inca 1463–1471

Topa Inca 1471–1493

Huayna Capac 1493–1527

13. *The map of the Inca conquest which made the realm of the Inca. From the compilations of Dr. John H. Rowe.*

within the framework of the Andes, and out of this discipline came the solid base of people, who, born to this type of society and thriving on it, went about the daily business of ordered human lives; and, in so doing, became an empire.

It took time to mold people in this manner, and its passage we must accept; and so we come to that period of Andean history (between the dates of A.D. 1200 and 1438) when their rulers, the "Incas," have pushed the expanding realm beyond the narrow confines of their "origin" valley and have established lordship over much of the surrounding mountains.

Within this Andean crucible the character of the people of the Incas was forged.

Part Two

THE PEOPLE

5 Appearance

THE QUECHUAS, the people of the Incas, were (it need hardly be stressed at this juncture) American Indians, and native to the Andes. Although there are, as anyone who has personally seen them, marked variations between the multifarious tribes strung out along the thousands of miles which are the Americas, there is an underlying appearance and trait in them all which is American. The Quechua was (or better *is*, since there remain some five million of them) of medium height and inclined to be thickset, with large hands, small wrists, a disproportionately large chest (developed for breathing in high altitudes), well-developed legs, and wide-spreading feet. They are broad-headed, with high cheekbones, prominent aquiline noses, and small, almond-shaped eyes.

The eyes appear to have a Mongolian tilt, actually produced by an epicanthic fold over the eye. This marks the American Indian and suggests as his remote ancestry a Stone Age migrant from somewhere out of Asia.

The women, as is natural, are smaller and more delicately constructed, yet they wear a false frailty for they are capable of arduous physical exertion; they give birth and return to the fields within twenty-four hours. Many of the Quechua women have delicate features; some could be called beautiful. At least the early Spaniards found them so and married them. The early Spanish portraits of them exhibit very delicate features, and a Spanish soldier, commenting on the women of Chachapoyas, wrote: "We found them the most fair and good-looking of any . . . seen in the Indies . . . exceedingly beautiful fair and well formed." [14]

Actually the Quechua's skin color runs from light chocolate to the color of beaten bronze, but to their conquerors, at first, they were all "brown and noisy." [49]

The factor which places the Peruvian really apart from many others is his physical stamina; he is capable of great physical endurance even in high altitudes—between 10,000 and 16,000 feet above sea level. This would make normal life impossible for most others.

He also has, remarks Harold Osborne, an exceedingly observant writer: "A high degree of physical insensibility which is [now] artificially enhanced by masticating the natural anaesthetic *coca* [see Medicine, Magic, and Curing, page 102] which renders him impervious to the effects of hunger, cold, exhaustion, and pain to an extent which is perhaps unequalled in another race."

Centuries of acclimatization in the Andes have developed his body so that he can, even in these antipodes, carry on normal functions. His chest, as well as his lungs, are abnormally developed so that the high altitude does not render him anoxic, his large lung capacity frees him from anoxemia (shortness of breath); he carries in his organism the hereditary and ancestral *soma* which allows life at these high altitudes.[44] However, it must be pointed out (so that one is not carried away by this uniqueness of the Andean man) that *physiologically* a 12,000-foot altitude in the Andes—for some reason not altogether clear—is equivalent to 6,000 feet in the Alps. And so, while at first the unacclimatized will suffer at these heights, time rapidly brings about an adjustment.

So it was this man, copper-colored, hard-working, tireless, robust, and by nature attuned to his surroundings, who became the broad base of the social pyramid which was the Inca Empire.

He was classified as a *hatun-runa* or *puric*,[64] an able-bodied worker; he belonged to an earth-cell commune, and as such was given a head count in the decimal pyramidal pattern of the Inca Empire.

6 Dress

THE DRESS of a *puric,* a man of the people, was simple and unpretentious. He wore a sort of poncho, much like a shortened version of a Victorian nightgown, made by folding a piece of cloth down the middle, cutting a slit for the head, and sewing up the edges, leaving a gap in the folds for the arms. This was called an *onka,* woven usually from the wool of the alpaca. He had another woolen cape garment (*yacolla*) which he threw over his shoulders at night or when the day was cold. This costume is well known, having been drawn by a native artist at the time of the conquest.

The last item of his dress was the breechclout; this was passed between his legs and the two ends held in place by a colorful woolen *chumpi* belt. He assumed this when he was fourteen years of age. Among those of mean birth, coming of age simply meant doing a man's business when he assumed the breechclout. Among the higher men, the *wara cicoy,* putting on the breechclout was a symbol of manhood and was attended with gaudy ceremonies.

So then, this breechclout, tunic, and rustic cape were all the Indian had to wrap his body in this frigid Andean clime. When working in the fields, he merely braided his long hair with colored woolen strings, but when traveling to a market or to a festival, he wore a distinctive headgear which distinguished him from other clansmen traveling on the royal road. On festive occasions he had a longer tunic, reaching to his ankles, on which he or his wife expended their finest talent; he usually went shod in *usuta* sandals.

Woman's dress was equally simple. It was a long rectangular piece of woven alpaca cloth (*anacu*) passed over the head and made wide enough to overlap and be held in place with a sash. It fell to the ankles, almost to her sandals. Over this she had another woolen cape garment woven from the wool of the alpaca, a *yacolla.* This she threw over her shoulders at night or when the day was cold. This costume is well known, having also been drawn by a native artist at the time of the conquest. Over her shoulders a shawl was held together by a copper, silver, or, if fortunate, a golden metal pin; this *topo* was universal with the women and still is. The hair was braided, bound, and tied with woolen ribbons, the ears pierced so as to hold copper, golden, or shell earplugs.

14. *A puric or* hatunruna, *an able-bodied worker of the Quechua tribe, dressed in festive clothes. Redrawn from Felipe Guamán Poma de Ayala (circa 1565).*

The men cut their hair in bangs with copper or obsidian knives; the women's hair was similarly treated, but hair styles differed from place to place and tribe to tribe, and were the most distinctive feature of the Indian. These variants in coiffure continued on direct order from their Inca; each *ayllu,* or clan, was to keep its distinctive hair style. They had small combs made of rows of thorns or polished jungle *chonta* wood.

The higher men and the "Incas by privilege," which included the governing *curacas,* dressed in a style similar to the common Indian, but the quality of the material was sumptuous. They were easily distinguished if not by their tunics then by the massive earplugs, usually in jeweled gold. The Inca himself dressed much as did his people except that his tunics were spun by his women attendants from the finest vicuña wool. While the man of the people seldom took off his tunic, the Inca never wore the same one twice. It was destroyed on the changing. "And I asked them why," wrote one of the soldiers. "They replied . . . because everything touched by the Inca-kings, who were children of the Sun, had to be burned and made to ashes and scattered to the winds so no one else could touch it." [49]

7 The Language

QUECHUA" was applied to the language of the people as well as to the Incas themselves. The word "Quechua" (it can also be written "Keshwa") means "warm-valley people"; in this sense it was the name of a tribe which lived in the *keshwa* grasslands. It is at once a geographical term, a region, a tribe, and a language. It is as a language, however —and written "Quechua"—that the word now has meaning.

The Quechua tribe originally lived in the region of Curahuasi, in a mild Andean climate close to the great canyon and river of the Apurimac. They were a large and dominant tribe when the Incas were still struggling in the Cuzco Valley.[53] After the Quechuas had been attacked by the powerful Chancas and deprived of their dominant position, the Incas moved in, took over the traditional Quechua territory, absorbed the people into their empire—and, presumably, took over the language.

It is not known what language the Incas spoke before this. After 1438 the Inca Pachacuti made Quechua his language. It then became the language of administration; every official had to know it. Teachers of Quechua went along with the conquests, so that gradually it superseded all the other bewildering number of native dialects. It is now spoken by whites and Indians alike in highland Peru; there is a variant of it in Ecuador, Colombia, Chile, and Argentina. It is a living language; there are many dictionaries of Quechua. It is a language of commerce as well as a literary one, and there are also musical records in Quechua. As a language it has marked characteristics and the closest related tongue morphologically is Aymara, but it doubtless is a part of a large language phylum.

The Incas had, as aforesaid, no writing. Their "literature" was transmitted orally and thus subject to the modification of the transmitter (see page 185), but it does not follow that because there was no writing Quechua had no grammatical rules. All the South American languages, even though they differ from one another, have rules of speech, but even to approximate the voice stops is a problem: the sibilant sounds and the fricative variants which give Quechua so expressive a sound have made it a problem to linguists, who have set

43

...own its voice sounds in varied orthography. There is considerable confusion in the writing of Quechua place names, towns, and gods.

Soon after the conquest, the Spaniards set about the task of preparing a vocabulary manual and a grammar, yet it was not until 1595 that the first Quechua grammar and vocabulary was published. Since that time many have been published; surprisingly enough, the most thorough and complete were done at varying dates in the nineteenth century by two physicians, one Swiss, J. J. von Tschudi, and the other German, E. W. Middendorf.

One of our foremost authorities on Inca culture has tried to explain the workings of the language in this way (an explanation seemingly far more complicated than the language itself): "A noun can be made from a verb merely by adding nominal suffixes instead of verbal suffixes to the stem, and the finest gradations of meaning can be expressed in inserting affixes between the stem and its grammatical ending." [40] In point of fact, Quechua has a very rigid phonetic pattern, yet it is at the same time plastic in its ability to make new word formations.

There is a surging emotion in the language, which doubtless comes from the fact that almost all Quechua words are accented on the penultimate syllable. It does not have the letters *b, d, f* and *j*, for example, but *p, t, v* and *h* take their place. There are guttural sounds, written *cc*, which are coughed up from the bottom of the throat, as the word *ccapac* (rich). There is a double *t* at the beginning of some words which is almost impossible for one to use unless he has long spoken Quechua; thus between *tanta* (a crowd) and *ttanta* (bread) there is a vast distance in thought and pronunciation.

Although it has no articles, Quechua has all the traffic of language: to form a plural the particle *cuna* was added.* The language has adjectives, genders, pronouns and verbs (*Cani,* "I am"; *Canqui,* "you are"; *Can,* "he is"), particles and adverbs. It is so complex that one wonders how a people could verbally, without writing, transmit so expressive a tongue.

To give something of its flavor an Inca chant would appear in this manner:

Caylla llapi	In this place
Pununqui.	Thou shalt sleep.
Chaupi tuta	Midnight
Hamusac.	I will come.

---

* In this book, however, *s* has been used in most cases, since *cuna* complicates an already complicated matter.

Whatever the grammar of the language (and it cannot be dwelt upon), Quechua was one of the instruments for carrying the Inca way of life throughout the length and breadth of the Andes, for by the Inca system of population transference (see The Organization and Assimilation of Conquered Lands, page 201), Quechua-speaking people were moved into newly conquered regions. This unification by language is one of the reasons why today more than 46.8 per cent of Peru's inhabitants speak Quechua, and why, in various dialects, it is heard throughout the Andes.

Quechua, then, whether it was traditional in his tribe or whether it was imposed upon him by conquest, was the communicative language of the *puric*.

8 *The* Ayllu

THE *ayllu* was the basic social unit, an early collectivist principle, which seems to have been indigenous throughout the Andean region. It was upon this *ayllu* principle that the Inca Empire was built.

The *ayllu* has been defined as a clan of extended families living together in a restricted area with a common sharing of land, animals, and crops so that everyone belonged to an *ayllu*. An Indian was born into it. This commune could be large or small, extending itself into a village or a large center (*marca*) or even into a complex city; for even Cuzco, the capital, was itself only an aggrandized *ayllu*. This social organization must be emphasized for the entire structure of the Inca society is based on it.

Individually no one owned land, it belonged to the community. The *ayllu* had a definite territory and those living within it were "loaned" as much land as was necessary for their well-being. Again, the Incas did not invent or create the *ayllu*—it was already there, part of the long development of primitive Andean society—but the Inca systematized and extended it. Everyone belonged to an *ayllu*. Each was ruled by an elected leader (*mallcu*) and guided by a council of old men (*amautas*) who, when asked, or even when not asked, gave their collective advice on matters affecting it. A number of these scattered communes came under the dominance of a district leader; these in turn formed a territory, and finally they coalesced into "one of the quarters of the world" which was ruled by a prefect (*apo*), who answered only to the Lord-Inca himself.

"The political pattern, and in turn the economic, can be described as a basically decimal pyramidal pattern. At the base of the pyramid was the *puric,* an able-bodied male worker. Ten workers were controlled by a straw boss [*cancha-camayoc*]; ten straw bosses had a foreman [*pachaca-curaca*]; ten foremen in turn had a supervisor, ideally the head of the village. The hierarchy continued in this fashion to the chief [*hono-curaca*] of the tribe, reportedly composed of ten thousand workers, to the governor of a province, to the ruler of one of the four quarters of the Inca empire, and finally to the emperor, the Sapa Inca, at the apex of the pyramid." [8]

For every 10,000 people there were 1,331 officials.

Normally an Indian, unless he died in battle in some far-away land or was transferred by orders, was born, matured, and buried in his *ayllu*; it was his primary and principal loyalty.

9 Marriage

AT THE AGE of twenty a man was expected to marry; if he did not, a woman was chosen for him. There seem not to have been, nor was there allowed to be, voluntary bachelors in the realm. While there is considerable detail on how the upper classes married, there is little or nothing on the common man. Marriage was motivated by economics rather than by abstract love. They did not have our own concept of prolonged wooing. If a man wanted a woman, he appeared with frequency at her father's house and joined in the work, and there were premarital sexual relations since absolute virginity was not overly important.

If a man did not find a woman, or the other way round, and had reached marriageable age, marriages were "arranged" during the visitation of the *tucui-ru-cuc*, the chieftain, "he-who-sees-all." Man and woman were arbitrarily selected as mates.

The marriage rites of the common Indians were simple: there was a joining of hands, later followed by a charming arcadian ceremony of an exchange of sandals. It must be understood that, though the life was hard, woman's lot here was no unequal concubinage, nor a weary servitude.

Marriage for the lower man was strictly monogamous, and since the woman prepared food and drink, the death of an Indian's mate was calamitous. Polygamy existed only for the nobility, the Inca himself having as many as seven hundred concubines. All of the ruling classes had plural wives. The first, however, always remained head wife; all the others were secondary. The death of a wife among those blissfully polygamous was not so difficult for the male, except that his secondary wives wept "noisily and lengthily" hoping by the attraction of sentiment to be upgraded to the position of head wife. Among the upper classes, sons of officials grew up with nurses their own ages who became their concubines until they were ripe for marriage, and orphan boys of the same class were often given to childless widows who instructed them in sex techniques and brought them up in exchange for this "servicing" of the old by the young. But none of this was within the reach of the common men; their lives were monogamous with little opportunity for variations on the theme of love. Their excessive sexual appetites, if any existed, were lost in the gross fatigue of ritually controlled labor.

Once a year, every autumn, the communal lands of the *ayllu* were divided among the members of the commune. Each couple united by marriage was given by the headman of the village, who presided over it, a *topo* of land, roughly 300 by 150 feet. The distribution of land was based on the amount of mouths to feed; those with larger families were given an increased acreage for each child. After the division, each family was responsible for its own particular piece of land.

The communal land of the *ayllu* was divided thus: first for the people, then for the Inca (that is the state), and thirdly for the Sun religion (call it tithes). Those two parts of the land for state and religion were tilled communally and harvested communally as part of the labor tax.

10 Domestic Architecture

THE INDIAN, with the mutual aid of his kin (*ayni*) within the commune, built his house. His house was, as it is now, a rectangular, windowless room built of field stone plastered with adobe mud or made up entirely of sun-dried adobe bricks. It had one entrance; the "door" was a woolen drapery. The supports which held up a roof, either gabled or hipped, were made from gnarled poles cut from mountain shrub. The roof was very thickly and beautifully thatched with *ichu* grass. The house had neither chimney nor fireplace; the smoke rising from the cooking was left to find its way out between interstices of the thatch. One can see the houses of rustic stonework at the fascinating ruins of Machu Picchu and observe very clearly this type of house. The floor was of beaten earth; perhaps skins of llamas or alpacas might have been laid upon it. There was no furniture; only the head of the tribe was allowed a stool. The Indian sat on the mud floor or on an old weaving, or squatted on his haunches. He slept on the ground either upon llama hides or on a blanket. Niches in the wall served as shrines for a local god. Pegs were used to hang extra tunics, robes, shawls, festive cloaks, slings, or if one belonged to a militia, a warrior's fighting tunic, helmet, shield, and distinguishing headgear with the totem mark of the village *ayllu*. Stones were arranged to hold up the clay cooking pots; the kitchen utensils, clay dishes for eating, copper or bronze knives, bone skewers, and a large stone mortar where the Indian women brayed their corn stuffs were in this section. All was simple and expedient.

The peasant's house (and one may here use the words "Indian" and "peasant" interchangeably) was rustically simple, yet the Inca architecture, which has excited so much attention, grew out of this type of house. Adobe, when ill-kept, has neither dignity nor grandeur, but when painted and thatched it can be, and undoubtedly was then, attractive. All architectural styles have had their roots in the homes of the peasants. The early rustic Greek or Roman peasant house was no better than this of the people of the Incas; those of the Iron Age in Britain were even ruder. Great architecture came out of all of these.

50

The houses might proliferate at random until the *ayllu* grew to be a *marca*. Then the village was built on a rectangular plan and laid out, presumably by professional architects sent out by the state. Three or four rectangular walls formed a sort of common wall, a *cancha,* a form of co-operative backyard; out of this grew the organized village. This type of architecture is still to be seen in the ruins of the village of Ollantaytambo under the fortress of the same name, which lies on the upper Urubamba River some twenty-four miles from Cuzco.

11 A Round of Daily Life

THE ROUND of daily life began at daybreak. The Indian *puric* slaked thirst and hunger by quaffing fermented *aka* (spoken of now as *chicha*), a mildly intoxicating, thick, malt-smelling beverage. A family had no breakfast as such; aside from *aka* the Indian ate what was left of yesterday's evening meal. Then he went to his fields.

The people were primarily farmers. With few exceptions all preliterate men in the Americas were tied to the earth; everything in the Inca culture must be understood in these terms. They were all members of an earth cell, and each thereby a symbiont of a soil community. After taking his *chicha,* he went to the fields, came back to eat at nine, then returned again to the fields. There he was joined by his wife and entire family; he labored all day in his fields.

The Indian, like agricultural people the world over, did not resent this incessant toil. His work as well as his relaxation was ritualistic and he would never have understood our separation of work and worship; for him, as Harold Osborne said: "Work that was not ceremonial lacked sense and meaning." "Unlike modern society," wrote Osborne, "in which work is regarded as a necessary evil undertaken to secure a leisure which society is untrained to utilize, in Inca society work was regarded as an end in itself."

In late midday the family gathered for their second meal. Cooking was mostly done by boiling; grease and frying were unknown. Corn was cooked with chili peppers and herbs until the corn split; this was *mote.* Sun-dried llama meat (*charqui*) was made into a soup into which *chuñu* (dehydrated potatoes, reduced to a thick whitish powder) was put to make a stew called *locro.* Popcorn was known and considered a delicacy. Ground corn was made into a paste and baked in the ashes like bread. Bright-eyed *cui* (guinea pigs), which ran about the darkened corners of the house, were raised for food. These types of food, certainly not inspiring to a gourmet, were, with variations, the food of the common Indian.

The evening and final meal was taken between four and five o'clock. Men squatted about the pots laid upon a cloth on the ground, helped themselves from the pot with fingers or quaffed the soup from ceramic bowls; the women sat outside of the circle, their backs to the men. When their *ayllu* was visited by the governor, the people of the commune joined together in long lines facing each other (all having brought their own food), and the *curaca* at the head of the "table" sat on his golden stool.

In the tropic latitudes night falls quickly. The door tapestry was lowered and all the members of the family sat upon the animal skins or cloths either about the coals of the pallid fire (for at these altitudes the fire is short-breathed), or about an open-mouthed ceramic brazier which gave out an exceedingly limited warmth. Fuel then, as now, was limited in the naked misery of the soil at 10,000 feet. There are few trees, only gnarled, low-lying scrub for their wood needs. They mostly used the dried *taquia* dung of the llama. The Indian had no artificial light beyond this. Night was spent listening to the oft-told tales of battle, of death, and of the little gods, and the father in these moments passed down to son the remembered things. Men repaired their tools, sharpened their bone knives, worked on weavings, or on the other things of their lives. Women labored quietly on the preparation of *aka*, the beverage that all drank. She first boiled the corn; then she put it into her mouth, chewed it, and in that process her saliva converted the starch, an enzyme distate, into sugar. The chewed mass was placed in a large pot and the enzymes further converted the malt sugar into dextrose, then into alcohol. The chewed corn mass was then mixed with water, boiled somewhat to add to the fermentation, and set aside for a day. The taste for this—to us a noisome beverage—must be acquired; certainly its gray color and heavily maltish odor of stale beer are not, as it was described by William Prescott, "sparkling *chicha*"—but it *was* their life. Women, when they did nothing else, were eternally preoccupied with it.

Cooking, as in almost all societies, was strictly woman's work. She, besides making the *chicha*, prepared all the food. It was her feet that crushed the liquid out of the potato, alternately frozen by the night and dried by the sun, forming *chuñu*. It was her hands which brayed the corn on the stone mortars, a type of millstone slab with ears for handgrips and made with a stone rocker quern for the grinding of corn, spices, and condiments. When woman was not preparing food, she was spinning; then and now it was the most common sight of the Andes—the Indian woman with wool distaff under her arm, walking that particular half-trot, half-walk, spinning the wool onto a straight spindle stick topped with a pottery whorl.

When the woman was not working in the fields or cooking or spinning, she was begetting; sterility was considered an abomination, and a man could leave his woman for it. The essential wealth of the empire, the Inca knew, was the people, and there were tribal rules about childbirth.

There are no precise details on children and childbearing, but need there be? Pleasures and pains are universal; amidst the eternal illusion that envelops us one thing is certain—suffering. It is the cornerstone of life. Before the birth of the child, the Indian woman went to the local *huaca* shrine and there prayed for a good birth. Both man and woman fasted.

After the birth the child was washed at the nearest stream, and on the fourth day placed in a cradle, called a *quirau*. It was carried on the mother's back and put always within easy reach. The child was suckled until two to three years of age, and then after that he began to imitate the parent's life. The child was not named for the first two years, being called nothing else than *wawa* (baby); then there was a family festival and the elaborate ceremony of *rutu-chicoy* (hair cutting) took place. The child was given only a temporary name, and the permanent name was given when he reached puberty.

An Indian's education was the mimicry of his parents in every act of their lives. Parents had no life apart from their children; all acts of their daily lives—eating, sleeping, and working—the children took part in. Sexual acts, too, were witnessed by the children, so that when a boy reached maturity he was in fact a miniature man.

At fourteen, a boy, having reached puberty, put on his breechclout. Among the peasant men it was a simple growing-up theme with all the broad ribald peasant humor reserved for such moments: the boy-turned-man then took his permanent name, either that of an uncle or of his father, or that of an animal.

It was far different with the sons of the upper classes: their putting on the breechclout meant a pilgrimage to the birthplace of the Inca state at Huanacauri up the Cuzco Valley, the sacrifice of llamas with priests officiating, and the smearing of blood on his face (our initiations into secret fraternities are not much different). Later he took on the aspect of a warrior, replete with shield, earplugs, and slingshot, and made public avowals to the Inca. Then the boy of the upper classes was given the type of traditional education which fitted him for a later administrative post within the realm.

Young girls became of age about the same time in a charming hair-combing ceremony, and they, too, took their permanent names; as befitting them their names were, in our sense, and I believe in theirs, somewhat poetic. One could take the name of a star and be called *Coyllur,* or that of the plant called coca, or a blue egg, and perhaps even *Ima Sumac* ("How beautiful").

Strangely enough, a woman, much different from lowly man, had a chance to leave the *ayllu* and better the existence into which she had been born. She could, if she had special talent in weaving, or grace, or was very beautiful, be selected

15. *Men and women, working together in teams, harvest potatoes. Redrawn from Felipe Guamán Poma de Ayala.*

as a "Chosen Woman" (*Nusta*). Under these conditions she was brought to Cuzco, or some other provincial capital of one of the quarters of the world, there to learn specific things such as weaving, cooking, and rituals of the Sun, the state religion. She might, as she usually did, become the wife of a high-placed official, or if fortune favored her, a concubine of the Lord-Inca himself.

But normally men and women of the realm of the Incas were born, reared, and buried within their *ayllu*. There was no escape from it. In this society a man was, in the words of Epictetus, "a factor necessary to complete the sum"; he was anonymous and communal. In this womb-to-tomb society everything was prescribed; work, love, festival, death. The price of this security was his absorption into the state.

Religion naturally played a great part in the Indian's daily round of life. The fundamental, enduring principle, the all-prevailing religious idea for this simple Indian was the *huaca*.

There are almost everywhere two aspects to religion. In its first aspect, it is the simple expression of natural man who faces the unexplainable and stands in awe of the supernatural and makes his obeisance to it. It has much to do with death, and among the Incas such fear was animated by the priests of the religion of the Sun; the simple Indian was frightened into a lugubrious phantasmagoria of illusions. And so he made his prayers and paid his homage. In its second aspect, the organized religion took his simple faith, here as in all other religions, and embroidered these fears with elaborate borders of hocus-pocus.

For the Indian the *huaca* was first the religion of the family, then of his *ayllu*—and then only lastly, that of the Sun, the state religion. He practiced the movingly simple rites of natural man. A prayer was offered up to the local *huaca* for the safe delivery of a child, or there was an invocation to the gods for a good harvest. There is a woman's prayer to the earth god to give the withheld gift of rain:

> *The most distressed of your children,*
> *The most distressed of your servants,*
> *With tears implores you*
> *Grant the miracle*
> *Of water,*
> *Grant the gift of rain*
> *To this unfortunate person,*
> *To this creature*
> *Pachacamac has created.*

The prayers to the gods which accompanied the offerings of first fruits were words well known to the head of the family. In primitive religions, power or spirit resided in everything, and the spirits had to be propitiated. *Huaca* was

16. *Woman opening the irrigation locks to water the fields. The artist shows an advanced form of irrigation reservoir. Redrawn from Felipe Guamán Poma de Ayala.*

animism and was what the Romans called *numen.* How could man mitigate the awe of this power and win for himself, his family, and his *ayllu* the peace of the gods? In this way the simple arcadian rites were practiced; only on great feast days did the common man see his prayers festooned with gaudy rituals by the priesthood.

Such, more or less, was the daily round of an Indian's life, a life which, if it were reduced to a moral platitude, could be summed up in one short sentence: *Ama sua, ama llulla, ama cheklla*—"Do not steal, do not lie, do not be lazy."

12 *Agriculture and Agricultural Origins*

THE STATE of mind of the Andean Indian, like that of the Roman peasant, was the mind of the farmer-soldier, not farmer, not soldier alone, but farmer-soldier. Although part of an agrarian militia, his life was based on agricultural routine. The caprice of weather might frustrate him and undo his work, but planting, growth, and harvest followed in appointed series.

He was a head count in the decimal system of classification, and a call for so many heads for war could take him from his fields and put him into battle, but no matter how grave the crisis, war was not his life rhythm. So deeply ingrained was this agricultural cadence that when the Inca, with his people, rebelled against their Spanish overlords in 1536 and subjected Cuzco to a terrible siege of sixteen months, it failed principally because of this. For even with his very way of life threatened if he did not succeed, still the farmer instincts dominated the soldier instincts and the uprising failed; the army melted away, demobilized so that the farmer-warriors could go back and cultivate their fields.

In the sense of the farmer-soldier, the Andean Indian must be understood.

Under the guidance of the Inca's "professionals," the whole of the realm—which included Andes, desert, and Upper Amazon—became a great center of plant domestication. *More than half of the foods that the world eats today were developed by these Andean farmers;* it has been estimated that more kinds of food and medicinal plants were systematically cultivated here than in any other sizable area of the world! One has only to mention the obvious: corn—that is, maize—(twenty varieties); potatoes (forty varieties); sweet potatoes, squash, beans of infinite variety; manioc (from which come our farina and tapioca); peanuts, cashews, pineapples, chocolate, avocados, tomatoes, peppers, papaya, strawberries, mulberries; so many and so varied the plants, and so long domesticated in the Old World, one forgets that all of these originated in the Americas.

The potato is dominant in the high Andes. Nowhere else

are there so many localized varieties or colors of potatoes as in Peru: white-yellow, pink-gray, brown, purple, black, spotted, and streaked; they are planted from the hot coast seemingly to the sky; the *tatu* variety is planted up to 15,000 feet above the level of the sea and is fully able to withstand the heavy frosts.

A member of the nightshade family, the potato was avoided by the European for three centuries because he believed it caused leprosy. In the seventh century the lowly "spud" was considered to be an aphrodisiac. The origin of potato (*papa* to the Incas) is so remote that its beginnings are lost in antiquity. Moreover, few plants have had the social influence of the potato.[55] Since it grew in the utmost livable heights of the Andes, it was the vegetable base of the Inca realm, but since the potato, unlike the other cultivated plants raised by the Andean farmers, was perishable, someone invented the *chuñu* process of potato preservation, and the Inca rulers systematized this by-product into an industry; in a large sense it prevented famine. *Chuñu* (pronounced "ch'un-yu") was the first really dehydrated food, and it was prepared in this manner: the potatoes were left outside to freeze, and on the following morning the people squeezed out the water with their feet. The process was repeated on five consecutive days. *Chuñu* may be preserved whole or made into a very white, light potato flour, and in this powdered dry state it can last for years. *Chuñu* was one of the principal foods stored in the public granaries throughout the Andes.

The grass we call "corn"—maize to the Mexicans, *sara* to the Incas—shared the social base with the potato, and it was, as now, the great food staple of the American Indian. The origin of corn is a fascinating botanical puzzle, and to the problem Dr. Paul Mangelsdorf and his associates in plant genetics have given much patient time.[39] Its place of origin is still unknown; "present evidence points to a dissemination in all directions of the early forms from an unknown center." Not able to withstand as harsh climate as the potato could, corn reaches its highest limits of cultivation in sheltered slopes about Lake Titicaca, at an altitude of 12,700 feet. *Sara* also has great antiquity; it is found in pre-Inca graves dating back to 3000 B.C.; it was even then fully matured as the Indian maize we know. The varieties are many. To the Incas, sweet corn is *choclo;* parching corn was *kollo-sara;* corn for the making of *chicha, saraaka;* corn for making a sort of hominy (*mote*) had kernels the size of hazelnuts.

These two staples were supplemented by quinoa (a pigweed, member of the goosefoot family), a tall reddish stalk, whose seed is much used as oatmeal is in the Scottish highlands, and *oca*, a tuberous plant which, like the potato, grows in the altiplano uplands. These four were the basic subsistence plants, although there were many more. In the warmer valleys, below 8,500 feet, a whole cornucopia of fruits and vegetables appeared: chili peppers, the principal condiment along with salt, tomatoes in considerable variety, beans (all world varieties except the European broad bean and the soybean), squash, pumpkins, wild gherkins, and fruits known and unknown to the world—papaya, chirimoya, avocado, guavas, and the granadilla, the fruit of the passionflower.

In the wet zones of the Montaña, the *yungas*, that part of the Upper Amazon under control of the Incas, peanuts, chocolate, two varieties of manioc, pineapples and soursop were cultivated—all of which originated in the Americas. And from the hot desert coast, fully under Inca control after A.D. 1450, came sweet potatoes, corn, squash and gourds, and a large variety of other plants long developed by the pre-Inca coastal peoples and immortalized in the realistic ceramics of the Mochicas, who existed between 400 B.C. and A.D. 800.

The archaeological world is today besieged by the "diffusionists" who once again (as has been done often in the past centuries) wish the Incas to come from some place else, much in the same manner as those who argue that Shakespeare could not have been Shakespeare. It is impossible for them to accept that indigenous man evolved culturally in this American world. Some claim that the Incas, unsatisfied with their vast Andean realms, went off into the Pacific on a fleet of balsa rafts and so colonized Polynesia; a contrary school suggests that the Incas owe their culture instead to the Polynesians, and to test it a raft was also launched in the opposite direction, that is, west to east. The Mayas must come from Angkor Vat, the Incas from China; the Hy-Brazilians, replete with alphabet, must be immigrants from the sunken continent—Atlantis.

Diffusion has long been known to be an essential dynamic factor in human culture. And it is agreed that many common cultural elements are due more to diffusion than to originality. In our own historical times we have seen how countries have benefited by borrowing—mostly through agricultural borrowing of domesticated plants.

But the Western Hemisphere, once it had its successive waves of migrants from somewhere out of Asia, was apparently sealed off by a geological transformation (as is equally evident in the diffusion of the primitive camel and llama

17. *Men and women working together, sowing the land. Note the difference in the* puric's *dress (see Figure 18). The first plowing then was festival; now work is at hand, and he wears common work dress. Redrawn from Felipe Guamán Poma de Ayala.*

from a common protocameloid ancestry from out of North America—see The Llamoids, page 74), and American man developed from man-as-animal into man-as-culture-bearer without any appreciable "outside" influence.

To show this, here is a comparative list of what man was using in the Old World and in the New in, say, 500 B.C.

EURASIA

1. *Green vegetables:* cabbage, lettuce, spinach, onion cucumber, egg plant, okra, asparagus, cress, garlic, artichoke
2. *Roots:* beet, parsnip, carrot, radish

3. *Fruit:* apple, pear, plum, cherry, grape, lemon, fig
4. *Nuts and oilseeds:* walnut, linseed, poppyseed, olive
5. *Legumes:* peas, lentils, soybean, broad bean
6. *Cereals:* wheat, barley, rye, oat, millet, rice
7. *Condiments:* mustard, cane sugar

INDUSTRIAL PLANTS:
1. *Vessel gourds*
2. *Fiber plants:* flax, hemp, cotton
3. *Dyestuffs:* madder, saffron, indigo

AMERICA

1. *Green vegetables:* cabbage palm, chayote
2. *Roots or tubers:* potatoes (many varieties), manioc, *camote, oca, olluco, añu*
3. *Fruit:* chirimoya, papaya, avocado, tomato, cacao (chocolate), pineapple, soursop, gherkin, strawberry, raspberry
4. *Nuts:* cashew, brazil, peanut, hickory
5. *Legumes: canigwa, tarwi, molle,* beans (all world varieties except European broad bean and soybean)
6. *Cereals:* maize
7. *Condiments:* peppers (chili—*aji*)
8. *Pseudo cereal:* quinoa
9. *Beverages:* mate, guayusa

INDUSTRIAL PLANTS:
1. *Rubber*
2. *Vessel gourds:* many varieties
3. *Fiber plants:* cabuya, cotton, etc.
4. *Dyestuffs:* cochineal, *achiote, genipa*

It will be immediately noticed that the two lists are almost completely different; only one item—cotton—is common to both continents, and that is wrapped in great mystery.

From the Fertile Crescent came wheat, rye, barley, and the pulses (leguminous plants with high protein content); wheat appears as early as 2500 B.C., and of course never appeared in the Americas until it was brought there by the Spaniard. Eurasia knew no beans other than the soy and the little-known broad bean, *Vicia faba,* descendant of a wild African variety; all other beans, no matter where they appear in the world, are American. White man, after the discovery of the Americas, was the intercontinental plant distributor; it was white man who brought tobacco, maize, tomatoes, chocolate, vanilla, strawberries, squash, potatoes, cranberries, pumpkin, red peppers (hence paprika), pineapples, papaya, and cashew nuts, to be cultivated in Europe and elsewhere. It was white man who brought the banana from Africa to the Americas in 1535, coffee from Mocha in Turkey in the late eighteeneth century, sugar cane from out of the Fertile Crescent to the tropics of America in the first days of its discovery; and rice. White man brought the pineapple to Hawaii, and in turn brought back, in one of the early voyages from the Philippines, the coconut—completely absent from the Americas. It is curious that in all the hypothetical diffusion contacts which play so great a part in the anthropological literature, the people of different continents did not make any plant exchange; they also forgot to bring to the Americas the vehicular wheel, the architectural arch, or the potter's wheel or the spinning wheel. In the matter of diseases, after the first contact, they did better; white man brought smallpox, the Indian gave him syphilis.

Cotton is the great puzzle, and it is riddled with mysteries. It was first cultivated in the Nile Valley after the fifth century B.C. The first exact date is 370 B.C., but Junius Bird, of the American Museum of Natural History in New York, found cotton in Peruvian graves which date back to 2000 B.C. At that early date, early Peruvian man cultivated cotton, spun and wove garments from it, and this *before it was cultivated by the Egyptians*. It was known to the Assyrians as "tree wool," yet the Greek etymology of the word points to the fact that it came originally from India.

Cotton as a botanical puzzle causes botanists genetic nightmares, for American varieties show that the chromosomes of cotton point to a trans-Pacific passage west to east by an Asiatic parent, an incompleted return movement of the tetraploid ancestry, which means that the "distributor" must have been birds if not man, who in the early history of the Americas "brought" cotton from the Old World, then several millennia later picked up the American cotton, which had developed new chromosome patterns, and brought it back again to Eurasia.[58] But what a thing to assign to birds, especially as birds do not eat the *Gossypium* seeds? And winds cannot distribute them for three thousand milles. Then, how to account for the same cotton, containing the same genes, in both continents?

Still, until someone presents us with something more positive than the accidental resemblance of sculpture between the Old World and New, it is safe to assume that man in America created his own culture without contact with the other continents, and if the American Indian shares, as he does, forty-nine cultural traits with the Polynesian, then it merely shows how severely limited the human animal is. In twelve thousand years he has been unable to think up another deadly sin. There are traits shared by the Tibetan living at 13,000 feet and the Inca living at the same altitudes —and why not? Geography itself is a determinant.

Agriculture was the soul of the Inca Empire; it determined everything. The Andean farmers' year was divided into two seasons: wet and dry. The wet season began in October and extended to May; the dry season, starting in May, although subject to considerable caprice (hence the Inca's preoccupation with obeisance to the unseen powers), continued into November.

In the autumn the lands of the commune were divided fairly between the members of the *ayllu*, the earth cell which controlled the communal land tenure. First the lands (*chacras*) assigned to the Inca, that is state lands, were cultivated communally (part of the Indians' *mita* tax of service), then the lands of the Sun, the state religion. The fruits thereof

18. *Men and women plowing the fields together. The men use the foot plow, called* taclla; *the women break up the clods of earth. Another woman brings corn* chicha *to drink. Redrawn from Felipe Guamán Poma de Ayala.*

were harvested and stored for the use of these agencies. These state granaries were stocked, so the early Spaniard remembered, with maize, quinoa, *chuñu, charqui* (dried llama meat), fish, cords, hemp, wool, cotton, sandals, and military arms, stored in hampers, each item in its appropriate warehouse. They were seen by Francisco de Xerez, the first soldier-chronicler of the conquest in 1533, who remembered these storehouses as being "piled to the roof, as the Merchants of Flanders and Medina make them." [76]

The work of tilling these fields done, the *puric* then turned to his own.

August was plowing time, and work in each other's field was—like all else—communal. It began with a festival. The nobility took it all most seriously and always participated. "If," wrote the Jesuit historian Padre Cobo, "the Inca himself or his governor or some high official happened to be present, he started the work with a golden digging stick which they brought to the Inca, and following his example all the other officials and nobles who accompanied him did the same." (No different in idea today than some state official turning the soil with a gold-plated shovel or else laying a cornerstone with a golden trowel.)

They had no plow as such, and no draft animals. Men used, as they still do, the *tacla,* or foot plow, which was a thick pole six feet in length with a fire-hardened point; sometimes it was bronze-tipped. There was a footrest near the tip and it was driven deep into the soil by a thrust of the foot and shoulder pressure. The clod of earth was then prized up. The digging stick, like all else in the realm, was a group tool and was seldom used by only one man. His kinsmen of the *ayllu* formed a long line across the field to be plowed, and with a rhythmic chant *"Jailli"* (pronounced "whaylyi," which means "triumph"), ". . . they triumphed over the soil," writes Garcilaso "the Inca plowing it and disemboweling it." The chant went something like this:

	Free translation
QHARICUNA:	THE MEN:
Ayau jailli, ayau jailli	Ho! Victory, ho! Victory,
Kayqa thajilla, kayqa suka!	Here digging stick, here the furrow!
Kayqa maki; Kayqa jumpi!	Here the sweat, here the toil!
WARMICUNA;	THE WOMEN (answering):
Ajailli, qhari, ajailli	Huzzah, men, huzzah!

The men worked backward, the women followed facing them and breaking up the clods with a sort of hoe called *lampa. Sara* (corn) was planted in September, potatoes when the rains began to fall, i.e., between October and November. After plowing the fields of the Inca, the Sun, and their own, they next turned to those fields of kinsmen who were serving in the army, and then finally to those of the sick and the halt. Their principal tribute (it was part of their tax), said Garcilaso, was "the working and cultivating and harvesting of the lands of the Sun and the Inca."

Agriculture was bound up very closely with terracing and irrigation, since the amount of flat land was severely limited and the Andean valleys are deep and narrow. The sides of the valleys were wonderfully terraced (see Plate VI), and these terraces are very exciting when seen for the first time. The rainy season run-off carries away soil; terracing prevented it. Terracing further extended the soil community where the earth surfaces were scant; so the Indians, too, were soil-makers.

Under Inca rule, terracing of the Andean valleys was a systematic part of their methods of soil preservation and soil creation. In the greater projects, those, for example, of Pisac —where the terraces stand poised over the heights of the Urubamba River—or at Ollantaytambo (where the workers cut into the living rock), professional architects were sent out from Cuzco to plan them. It was an enormous expenditure of labor. That these terraces still stand after five centuries is sufficient testimony to the foresight of those Inca rulers.

Irrigation was tied closely with terracing and so naturally with agriculture. It was the lifeblood of empire. In the wet season rain does not always fall nor does all this borax-filled earth hold the water, so irrigation was the answer, and the Inca engineers harnessed the brawling streams pouring out of glaciers and brought them down in the most careful manner to water fields, even though separated by immense distances from the watercourse. These techniques helped to control the density of population and gave the social body a meticulous balance between population and productivity. Much Inca-directed skill was devoted to irrigation. There were immense water reservoirs in the fortress of Sacsahuamán above Cuzco; water was laid underground in superbly made stone-laid sewers in many widely spaced areas. Rivers were straightened, canalized as one sees the Urubamba River, a few miles east of Cuzco and below the great fortress of Pisac. This type of advanced engineering once extended throughout the empire, but is now only dimly seen since so much has been lost to the insults of time.

Irrigation techniques are inseparable from a developed agriculture, and their elaboration marked man as a settler, brought about a corporate life with settled habits; irrigation also created the city-state.

Irrigation, it need hardly be said, was not an Inca invention, but it *was* an Inca perfection. On the desert coast the Mochicas, to mention one great pre-Inca dynasty, had vast irrigation works, and their heirs, the Chimús, built their cities on the ruins of those of the Mochicas and extended the irrigation system so that their cities were supplied by gigantic stone-laid reservoirs. In the Ica-Nazca coastal regions, west of Cuzco on the Pacific Ocean, these cultures, between the years A.D. 500–800, also elaborated immense irrigation works; the underground reservoirs are still known as *puquios*. Of all this, the Incas were the inheritors.

Yet under the Incas terracing was perfected and extended. Water was so engineered as to be introduced at the top of the terraces, thence it ran down from one gigantic terraced step to another, the whole area being watered by a single stream. Water conduction demands careful design and must be determined by a knowledge of hydrologic conditions, the nature of the soil, and the general conformation of the land. To secure the flow it must run down a slight incline: too fast, it will erode the banks; too slow, it will allow weeds to grow and silt will choke up the channels. It is scarcely curious that wherever in this variegated globe water conduction has been practiced, the techniques of it are almost identical. In ancient Mesopotamia, after its conquest by Hammurabi in 1760 B.C., land exploitation was centralized, which led naturally to the erection of canals, reservoirs, and irrigation dikes.[61] King Hammurabi's "Water Code" is written in a form that sounds like an Inca text: "Each man must keep his part of the dyke in repair." Royal letters were dispatched to governors giving them over-all responsibility to keep the waterways open and the dikes in repair: "Summon the people who hold the fields on the side of the Damanu Canal that they may scour it."

This is only one instance of parallelism in human inventions, for after all it is the stomach that is the all-compelling motive of invention, and man through his ages tested, tasted, and tried the fruits and grains that fell within his ken; he learned to evaluate them, select and plant them—for this reason one need not become unduly overexcited about the parallelism of means and methods in terracing used by peoples out of contact, for where geographical conditions are similar, agricultural methods and water induction will also spring up naturally. One need not fall back on diffusion as an explanation. The peasant is landbound. He may be a Peruvian *puric* or an Egyptian *fellah,* but he remains the "eternal man." He is, in the Spenglerian dictum: "the eternal man, independent of every culture that ensconces itself in the cities. He precedes it, outlives it: a dumb creature propagating himself from generation to generation, soil bound, a mystical soul, a dry, shrewd understanding that sticks to practical aptitudes."

19. *The drum was a part of the festival in which tribesmen imitated the things of their lives. The men are dressed as birds. Redrawn from Felipe Guamán Poma de Ayala.*

In Peru, after the September planting, especially in those lands unreached by irrigation, October was always the "critical" month; if rain did not fall, there would be a crop failure. In instances of prolonged drought the Indian fell back on the "mysteries" and the high priests took over.

Throughout the planted land llamas were sacrificed to

the rain gods. If that did not seed the rain clouds, then a man, a woman, perhaps even a child, was sacrificed. The procedure was repeated in Cuzco on a greater scale. The people paraded dressed in mourning; black llamas were tied without food or drink in the belief that the gods could not withstand the plaintive wail of the llama and would send rain to assuage it.

When the corn was ripe, the Indians faced another crisis: birds and animals in the Andes converged on the grain to get at it before it was harvested. Boys, disguised with wolves' skins over their heads, waited to plague birds with sling-shots; at night women stayed up to beat on a small drum. Everything, it seemed, conspired against the Indian.

When the crops survived all of this, then there occurred the corn harvest festival; all joined together in the field, and that part of the grain that would not be immediately consumed was stored in the public granaries.

It was after this that the Incas offered the first fruits to their local shrine—the *huaca.*

The idea of the *huaca* is intimately bound up with religion; it combines that which is magical and charm-bearing. *Huacas* were varied and numerous. A *huaca* could be a natural feature of land, a mountain crag; rivers were *huacas,* such as the Apurimac, "the Great Speaker," over which the Incas hung their greatest suspension bridge; and *huacas* were lakes, springs, or other natural objects. All were worshiped in one form or another. But since religion was practical and life was religion, agriculture as such was holy too, and any ritual connected with it was *huaca.*

The best-known and incontestable *huacas* were those built in the fields; they are still to be seen throughout the Peruvian coast. Some near Lima contained upward of twelve million individual bricks. They began, certainly, as a stone deposit; as an Indian worked the fields he tossed stones onto a common pile. This became a shrine and was formed into a stepped pyramid, as most *huacas* are built. Then on top was added a gaudy canopy, where a wooden or stone effigy was placed. That was the *huaca:* "a primordial synthesis in which the conceptual differences of content have never been made analytically distinct." [46]

These *huacas* erected in the people's fields were the primary source of religious expression of the people. Here the first fruits of the harvest were laid. The *huaca* is certainly not wholly Inca nor is it exclusively American; the farmers cultivating their soil, as in Mesopotamia, built their shrines, called *Tells,* more or less in the same manner, and they were placed in the wheat fields. The Sumerian civilizations in the

fertile Tigris-Euphrates delta believed also that they, as
farmers, were dependent on the favor of the deities, and to
secure, to maintain these favors, such as rain and sun, they
paid tributes from their first produce in quite the same manner. Human beings everywhere act like human beings. They
knew that the gods were dead, but they persuaded themselves that they were living and fell, just as we ourselves do,
into inextricable contradictions.

20. *When the corn is ripe, everything conspires against its harvest.
A boy protected by a wolf's skin kills animals and birds with his sling.
Redrawn from Felipe Guamán Poma de Ayala.*

13 MITA: The Service Tax

DEATH AND TAXES are not a modern preoccupation; they were just as inevitable if one lived under the rule of the Incas. Since they did not have money, that "great human convenience, the Indians' taxes were in service, called *mita*.

Money began in Babylonia, where it was at first a thin golden ribbon that could be told out from a wheel attached to a wall, but the "eternal man," the farmer who lived away from city cultures, kept firmly to the barter system. The primitive Romans—the pastoral folk—reckoned their values in cattle; the very word money, writes R. H. Barrows, was *pecunia* (whence "pecuniary," from *pecuniarius* which means "head of cattle").

The Incas, even if they did not have money, had value; value here was work performance.

The first *mita* of the *puric,* the common taxpayer, was, as already noted, paid in the form of agricultural service, which consisted of a communal cultivation of fields assigned to the Inca and the Sun, the harvesting of the crops, and their storage and attendance. The other form of *mita* was work on government-controlled projects (a similar system was set up under the German National Socialist government as *Arbeitsdienst*).

Each taxpayer was obligated to give a stated amount of work annually to the government. It might be as a laborer in the mines (an odious service which all resented, and the Inca recognized it by rotating the miners rapidly), on roads, or in bridgebuilding or the building of temples or fortresses under professionals (i.e., non-taxpaying individuals, architects)—or any other of the multiple services that a fully organized state needed. There was a constant need of specially trained runners for the *chasqui* courier service.

All labor levies were based on the decimal classification. If one thousand Indians were needed to repair, say, a suspension bridge which would mean cutting cabuya fibers, spinning thick cables, and suspending them across an abyss, then each leader of a given *ayllu* would be asked to furnish one hundred Indians. Within the space of time it took for the courier to arrive with his instructions, the men would be gathered and marched off to the task. Accurate records of service for each community were kept on the knot-string record (see The Knot-String Record, page 185).

Some communities had a permanent service. The village of Curahuasi, which is still extant, lay closest to the great suspension bridge, the Huaca *chaca* (so wonderfully described by Thornton Wilder in his *Bridge of San Luis Rey*), which hung across the Apurimac gorge. Its *mita* was the upkeep of that bridge, the restringing of the cables every two years. So ingrained was this system that even during three hundred years of Spanish occupation, even into the republican period of Peru, the village of Curahuasi performed that task; they strung the suspension ropes, three hundred feet long, for the last time in 1879.

Mita could be paid in transport of military equipment or by service as litter bearers (see Chapter 30, Transport). To appreciate how organized was the *mita* service system, when the great fortress of Sacsahuamán was begun circa A.D. 1438 to defend Cuzco from attack, upward of thirty thousand Indians were set to work quarrying, dressing, and putting into place the gigantic megaliths. It took labor shifts of thirty thousand Indians eighty years to build this structure—a work which ranks in scale with the pyramids.

The small professional class (other than the Inca and his enormous family, who were in effect the administrators of the realm, the *curacas,* or governors, the "Incas by privilege") was made up of the bodyguards of the Inca (who were in effect a cadre of warriors), accountants (*quipu-camayoc*), silversmiths, tapestry weavers (all had titles of their craft), the architect-engineers, and, of course, the priests, as always and as everywhere; none of these paid *mita*. But all others of the millions who formed the realm did. The *mita* tax seems to have been administered fairly and seems not to have been resented by the Indian. Pedro de Cieza de León, writing in 1550, explains how when the Inca wanted to determine what tribute was due from all the provinces between Cuzco and Chile, he dispatched his governors along with the account keepers. They went from village to village examining the condition of the people and their capacity for payment. An inventory, kept on the colored strings of the *quipu,* recorded the various products: the number of heads of llamas, the number of taxpayers, and the quantity of metals, for the Inca automatically owned all the gold and silver of the realm. This done, they returned to Cuzco with the reigning chieftains, and so with *quipu* in hand and his governors to interpret them, the Inca "addressed them lovingly saying that as they received him as their sole lord . . . they should take it in good part and without feeling it burdensome, to give the tribute that was due to his royal person. . . . Having been answered in conformity with his wishes, the lords of provinces returned to their lands, accompanied by the Inca's people who fixed the tribute." [14]

Since the Indian paid his taxes in time rather than in money, it is fully obvious why laziness was a capital offense. For, wrote William Prescott (1847) in his immortal and still largely valid *Conquest of Peru:* "The whole duty of defraying the expense of government belonged to the people . . . Even his time he could not properly call his own. Without money, with little property of any kind, he paid his taxes in labor. No wonder that the government should punish sloth with death. It was a crime against the state and to be wasteful of time was, in a manner, to rob the exchequer."

Yet the *mita* system did not seem burdensome to the Indians themselves; they were happily content in work so long as it was ritualistically controlled, and since there was no ambition to accumulate wealth by surplus production, all the work they did for the state came back to them later when famine made them fall back on the stores in the public granaries—the direct result of their *mita* tax.

Such were the advantages of a womb-to-tomb society; its disadvantages will appear later.

14 The Llamoids: Llama, Alpaca, Vicuña, Guanaco

THE AMERICAN Indian did not have, it scarcely has to be repeated, draft animals of any form. Outside of woman, who was the first carrier, the closest that indigenous man got to a domesticated animal was the llama. Before the coming of the white man, America had neither horse, nor steer, nor bovines of any form, nor domesticated pigs or goats. The only animal, and it was not a draft animal since the vehicular wheel did not exist in prehistoric America, was the llama and its wool-bearing relatives.

The llama is the most stylized animal in nature's book; it has a camel's head, large eyes, a split nose, a harelip, no upper teeth, and two-toed feet, which look cloven but are not. Its usual gait is as leisurely as that of a *grande dame* entering a salon, but it can leap like a deer, and when it stampedes it runs as fast as a train (an Andean train).

Along with its remote ancestor the camel, it has (at least for the subject of this book), an amazing history. As far as is known now, the animals known to us as camels and llamoids (which include the llamas, guanacos, alpacas, and vicuñas), originated out of the proto-cameloids who were the dominant types in the Eocene period of geologic time. The particular group which, it is believed, gave rise to the present-day llamas and camels has been found only in North America. Due to the increasing aridity and a floral change which affected the food supply, there was during Tertiary times a continual faunal readjustment through migration. Associated with the proto-camels are rhinos, and particularly tapirs, which are found today only in Malaya and Central and South America.

These, like the *Protylopus* which had camel-like features, in that geological epoch preceding the appearance of man, must have followed a land bridge that most likely connected the roof of America—Bering Strait—with Outer Mongolia. Whatever the "missing links," that animal which was to evolve into both camel and llama appeared in North America in the Lower Eocene times, was forced by the "general floristic change affecting the food supply of herbivorous groups" [22] into migration out of its origin zone: one offshoot moved south into South America and became the llamoids, others moved into Mongolia and became in time the well-known dromedary camel (of one hump) and the Asian (or Bactrian) with two.

The llamas are cameloids: they differ in lack of hump, sternal knee, and hock callouses; the camels grow to a weight of twenty-two hundred pounds, the llama to, at best, four hundred. Their relationship to man, his cultures, and the highways he constructed on differing continents is amazingly similar.

Nobody knows when the first camel appeared in the recorded history of man. There are no records of any in a wild state, yet they have a longer heredity of variation and adaptation than any of the cattle. They do not appear on the early monuments of Egypt, and Julian Huxley has recently confirmed [30] that they did not appear in Egypt until 300 B.C. Camels were apparently still relatively new to the Fertile Crescent since when Xerxes in 480 B.C. started on his invasion of Greece, Herodotus says, that vast army had only one camel corps: "The Arabians equipped . . . on riding camels which in speed are not inferior to horses," but they "brought up the rear to avoid spreading panic amongst the horses who cannot endure the presence of camels."

Camels apparently did not appear in North Africa until late Roman times: at least Sallust says the first time Romans saw camels was in Asia Minor when they were fighting Mithridates (which would be 88–84 B.C.), and Julian Huxley affirms that they were not abundant there until the fourth century A.D. Yet camels formed the main transport along the ancient Silk roads, just as llamas formed the transport on the highways of the Inca.

The camel was the first boxcar. And more; it is a veritable walking commissariat; alive and dead it contains almost everything useful to man. Its wool is made into the "black tents"; [16] its meat is tender. The camel only walks and gallops; fully loaded, up to fifteen hundred pounds, it can travel twenty-five to twenty-eight miles a day. When urged to gallop it can move at the speed of an express train, and it outstrips a horse traveling one hundred miles a day. Its paunch holds enough water for days (it can be drunk by man in dire emergency); it has trapdoor nostrils to keep out the sand drift, and its great liquid eyes are so heavily lashed that not a grain of sand can enter in during the wildest windstorms. There is something *right* about a camel; it can withstand the temperature of the Gobi Desert at 140 degrees and also be impervious to Arctic cold. The camel, says the author of

Travels in Arabia Deserta, can be "clothed on the high days with glorious pall of green velvet" with a seat of a four-poster litter and march through the empty way of the desert, or it can lie for weeks in the spring pastures "laying up flesh and grease in their humps for the languor of the desert summer." [16]

Whatever one says about the camel one can say about the llama: it furnishes food, wool, transport, and fuel; it is a social beast, i.e., although it has no love of mankind such as horses and dogs display, none the less it is part of man and his society.

After twelve months of gestation the camel cow gives birth to a calf "as big as a grown man," observed Charles Doughty; "the herdsman stretches out the newly-born's legs, draws it out of the womb, claps it on the chest, revives it, and within three hours it stands, suckles, and gives first voice, sheeplike in complaint." After that the camel cow will yield three pints of milk daily (the llama was never milked). Like the llamas, the camels have no upper teeth after they mature; grass, thorny boughs of sweet mimosa leaves are ripped off by a stiff upper lip. Since there is little fuel in the desert lands of the camel, its dung, called *jella,* is used as fuel. When overburdened, camels will protest the vast bulk with a groan but march to the end in silent fortitude.

They give everything—even their urine, which is used by the nomads to wash their babies in the belief that the odor will keep away insects. Resigned, unreproachful, uncomplain-

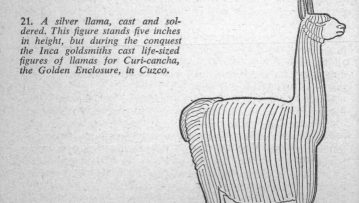

21. *A silver llama, cast and soldered. This figure stands five inches in height, but during the conquest the Inca goldsmiths cast life-sized figures of llamas for Curi-cancha, the Golden Enclosure, in Cuzco.*

ing, the camel goes plowing across the vacant land, with the nomad women walking barefooted, spinning, beside their slow-pacing camels. A camel is like some graceful, hideous woman, someone wrote, who has magic in her way of walking—like Baudelaire's courtesan: "worn-out, heroic . . . the indestructible elegance in her."

Whoever says "camel" says "llama," for in all or almost all of their habits tied to man they are comparable even though distant by a hundred thousand years of variant evolution; both are man's transports along some of the most extraordinary roads built by him. The llama mimics the camel except for bulk, but their mechanism of water storage, even without the hump, is quite the same (metabolism of subcutaneous fat and body carbohydrates). They are seldom ridden, although there are Mochica ceramics showing Indians mounting llamas; they are not milked and never used for wheeled drayage. Yet they have, like the camel, that amazing plastic ability for adaptation; they can live in the range of perpetual glaciers, 17,000 feet altitude, or acclimatize themselves to the desert. The Mochicas (A.D. 400–800), in their pottery show them carrying heavy loads through the desert, with a woolen fringe over their eyes to keep down the glare of the sun. Normally a llama loaded with half its weight will walk between six and twelve miles a day; if pressed it will travel longer. As the camel was to the Asian, so the llama was to the Inca; its wool was used mostly for heavy blankets, strong cords, sacks for cargo (the wool is very greasy); its meat was made into sun-dried *charqui* (hence our western word "jerky"); its dung, *taquia*, like that of the camel, was a fuel, and was gathered in their communal voiding places.

To have been a llama herdsman in Inca times was a complex and honored profession, since the llama not only yielded all material things, but its lungs were consulted in times of dire stress for the omens they would reveal, just as the Romans consulted chickens' entrails.

The Incas, it need hardly be said, did not "invent" the llama; it was present in Peruvian culture twenty-five hundred years before the Incas even appeared; it is so old that it appears mummified in Paracas graves, where it has five toes instead of two! But the Incas did systematize llama husbandry.

There now seems little doubt that the untamed guanaco is the wild progenitor of the llama; the llama itself is a hybrid, but these two are most closely related. Of the other two of the llamoids, the alpaca, which now, as it did during Inca times, furnishes wool for weaving, seems to be a hybrid

of the llama and the vicuña. The alpaca does not "carry";
it is not much larger than a large sheep and is confined
mostly to the altiplano, about 15,000 feet altitude. The vicuña (pronounced "ve-kuhn-ya"), the most delicate of the
llamoids, is completely wild. "A delicate animal with plenty
of fine wool," said Cieza de León, ". . . it stands higher than
a goat and the color of its whole is clear chestnut. They are
so fleet that no dog can overtake them and they frequent the
loftiest fastnesses near the line of snow." Possessing the finest
wool in the world (worthy of Jason's Golden Fleece), the
vicuña was taboo to ordinary man: only the Inca and his
circle might wear garments from its wool. They were obtained in hunts, as Cieza de León explains: "When the Yncas
desired a royal hunt, they ordered three, four, ten thousand,
twenty thousand Indians to surround a wide track of country
and gradually converge until they could join hands . . . They
made very precious cloth from the wool of the vicuñas for
the use of the Ynca." Very often, "there were as many as
forty thousand head of guanacos and vicuñas alone in this
great circle; most of the female vicuñas and some of the
males were released, but they were shorn of their wool before they were allowed to go free . . . that of the vicuñas, as
fine as silk, was reserved for the Ynca's service."

For transport during war, for carriers of trade goods during peace, the Incas depended mainly on the llama. It was
the principal pack animal (outside of the Indian himself),
and in conquests thousands were used along the ways of the
Incas.

The llama herds were an integral part of Inca economy.
Each *ayllu,* or earth cell, had its own contingent of llama
herds, which were counted by the *quipu-camayoc*—the knot-
string-record accountants—so the Inca could know the precise number of llamas within his realm; they reached, if we
are to believe the chroniclers, into the hundreds of thousands.

As llamas are a hybrid, the Indians had to give them constant attention during the reproductive act; the males were
aided during copulation and Indians were on hand to aid
the birth of the single llama calf given at issue. Because of
this intimacy a considerable folklore has grown up about the
llama: one, that as the Indian found the female llama attractive, a male herder must always have his wife present
during his chore. Then, since *all* anthropologists (if not all
physicians) agree that syphilis was American in origin, and
that it had never appeared in the Old World until Columbus
returned to Spain after his first voyage, it was presumed by
some that this disease came from the llamas and that In-

dians must have practiced zoophily (literally: love with an animal). The supposed result was syphilis. And this was transmitted to white men. It is good folklore but not good science: no llama was ever found to harbor *Treponema pallidum*, the spirochete of syphilis. Which fact does not ruin the theory of this social disease as originating in the Americas, but only disposes of the llama as the original carrier. What is it that Herbert Spencer said when he excused himself for bringing up an ugly fact to ruin a beautiful theory?

15 The Loom — Weaving of Wool and Cotton

THE WEAVING skills occupied both men and women. The wool stuffs collected by their *ayllu* were divided among them according to their needs, i.e., depending on the number and demands of each member of the commune. The residue was stored in the official storage bins, the precise amounts accounted for by those officials who recorded this on their *quipu* string counters, so that the governor of a given province could know precisely down to the last fiber how much wool was available in this district.

Wool, until Inca conquests opened up the channels for trade to obtain cotton fiber, was *the* Andean material. The wool of the alpaca, generally white, but mixed with grays and natural browns, was used for wearing apparel because of its superior fineness and long fiber; llama wool, coarse and greasy, was spun, in a distinctive brown-white color, as fiber for heavy blankets, durable sacks for llama transport, and ropes and llama halters. Vicuña, soft, silky, the finest in the world, was reserved only for the highest, luxury weaving. The wool was dyed before carding and spinning, although where the particular weaving called for the natural colors of the wool they were fully utilized.

"Virtually nothing is known of the dyeing procedures," writes Junius Bird,[9] the most experienced of America's "dirt archaeologists." This is surprising since the pre-Inca graves of Paracas have yielded so fantastic a collection of weaving techniques and colorings that one textile expert distinguished 190 hues! Mordants, metallic substances such as copper and tin, were definitely used to give permanence to vegetable dyes; *achiote* is a tree whose pod yields a red dye, the genipa, a jungle pod which yields a jet black, and the seed of the avocado long has been known to have yielded a permanent bluish dye; one recent experimenter extended to 250 the number of plants from which good dyes could be obtained in Peru. In Mexico, they used the cochineal, a scale-insect parasite (*Coccus cacti*), but this seems to have been absent in Peru. The wool dyers certainly made use of a shell-fish dye, just as the people of the Mediterranean obtained the famous *purpura* and *murex*—the Tyrian purple—from the molluscs of the island sea.

After dyeing, the wool was tied to a distaff and spun. The spindle was a straight stick with a piece of ceramic whorl (usually nicely decorated) which one spun between the fingers as one would a top, while the other fingers, well moistened with spittle, fed the fibers from the wool ball on the distaff. This system of spinning is world-wide. The spindle whorls found in Palestine or in Egypt as early as 3000 B.C., or in Troy of the same period, are so similar in design and purpose that, placed beside those found in Peru dating from the same time-epoch, they can hardly be told apart.

Cotton was spun in the same manner. As is well understood, the Inca people were out of the range of cotton; but by trade and barter they secured it from the Upper Amazon, famous for a long-stapled naturally brown cotton, and from the coast where it was extensively planted.

Tree cotton was known in India as early as 3000 B.C., and is mentioned in the writings of Herodotus. Presumably the cotton stalk plants as grown today were not those cultivated by the ancient Peruvians; rather they were "cotton trees." When cotton, through extensive trade, came to the Incas, they used it for certain weavings with considerable eagerness; it has, since its early cultivation on both continents, Old and New, been an important fiber because it is so easily processed. The things that these people could do with handspun cotton are utterly amazing: it could be gauzy tissue, or a gossamer of muslins of extraordinary whiteness and thinness (mummies on the coast were wrapped in it); guilds of cotton weavers were attached to the Peruvian coastal temples just as factories of cotton weavers were connected with temples in Egypt.

The looms to spin wool and cotton were of three kinds: the backstrap or belt loom, wherein the upper part is tied to a tree or upright and the belt for tension is passed around the back of the weaver (hence the name); the horizontal loom, put upon the ground, the warp being supported by a forked-stick support a foot above the ground; and the vertical loom, built against the wall, upon the cloth of which the weavers—usually men—worked standing. "As yet," says an authority, "no one has made a comprehensive study of the loom types still in use and of their distribution in Peru." [9]

What is certain is that the art of the loom was widespread throughout Peru, and that the Incas were inheritors of the techniques that had been thousands of years in the perfecting. Almost all authorities seem to agree that most of the fabrics found in graves came from the backstrap loom; these looms have often been found in graves—usually in that of a woman so that in the netherworld she could occupy herself as she had in this one—and on these backstrap looms cloth is found half completed. By comparing these with the present-day looms of tradition-bound Peruvian communities, one can see that the techniques have changed little in two thousand years.

Weaving has had a long history in Peru; the most advanced was that produced by that unknown people called Paracas, on the desert coast of southern Peru. From this culture (which endured with some interruption between 400 B.C. and A.D. 400) have come pieces of embroidery and weaving which are admitted to be without peer in the world. The prodigious expenditure of time to weave so complex and startling an array of ponchos, turbans, shawls, skirts—all for the dead—is quite incalculable; the designs, the craftsmanship, are amazingly consistent.

On the north coast, five hundred miles from the Paracas, the Mochicas, whose culture extended from A.D. 400 to 800, pushed weaving to such perfection that it seems to have been done on a factory principle. At least a celebrated Mochica ceramic exhibits a row of women (all with backstrap looms) weaving industriously, while a male supervisor sits under a sunshade and directs them. So the Incas inherited complete techniques; their notable contribution was to perfect a method of obtaining the wool of the vicuña which was made, as said elsewhere, into weavings of such fineness that they were mistaken by the first Spaniards to be of heavy silk.

As in spinning, so with looms (*ahuanas*). Those used by the ancient Peruvians are identical with those of other civilizations with which they had absolutely no contact. A form of backstrap loom was used in Egypt, a horizontal loom appears in predynastic Egypt, and the one pictured on the tomb of Khnem-hotep (at Beni Hasan), circa 1900 B.C., is identical with those of the Andean and coastal Peruvians. The same may be said of the vertical looms which appear in the tomb of Thotnefer at Thebes: in form and function they are quite similar. Man is like the earth, repetitious in form. As Charles Doughty had it, "The carcass of the planet is alike everywhere; it is but the outward clothing that is diverse."

The weaving methods of the Incas, like all else about them, were functional. Three grades of wool cloth, all distinguished by names, were woven. The common was *awaka* woven material. The finest and most finished (on both sides) was *kumpi*. Many Inca materials were done in tapestry

22. *Woman weaving at a backstrap loom. This was the common type of loom throughout the Americas. It is still used. Redrawn from Felipe Guamán Poma de Ayala.*

weave, but much of this has perished due to the climate. The thick and heavy weave, *chusi,* was a baizelike material used for bed or floor coverings. The looms on which the finest *kumpi* materials were woven were ". . . made on frames of considerable size, the function of the lateral beams being to give rigidity and a proper tautness to the warp. There were no needles in these frames, all the work being done by the weaver's fingers and by the spindles or bobbins carrying the colored weft-threads which were beaten up after insertion by the use of the weave dagger." [41]

Men were weavers (*kumpi-camayoc*) as well as women; the latter, however, were entrusted with the finest wools of the alpaca and the vicuña. One of the functions of the Chosen Women was to produce the fabulous vicuña tunics for the Inca—the kind which he never wore more than once before it was destroyed. They also fashioned the feather tunics, a mosaic of jungle-bird feathers put quill-first into the warp of the weaving. "The luster, splendour and sheen of the fabrics of feather-work," said the Jesuit Bernabé Cobo, "were of such beauty that it is impossible to make them understood, unless by showing them," and what he said then applies equally now. They are indescribable except to call them feather mosaics. In addition to the feather weaving, other

cloth was richly adorned with bangles of gold or tiny bells
and golden particles called *chaquira;* there were tunics completely covered with gold, silver, or burnished copper pieces.
I can go no further except to urge those near a museum to
seek them out.

Now if the Indian was an automaton in all else, he seems
to have been allowed full freedom in design for his weavings.
The selection of bright and vigorous colors is bold and startling; here the weavers have achieved an effect of heightened
colorfulness by discords of adjacent hues, the kind of color
effect which was developed by Gauguin and a few other post-
impressionist painters. Each weaver, presumably, selected his
or her colors and designs so fanciful that they seemed to
come as a protest to the confined circle of his life. Having
been allowed full individuality, the weaver made the most
of it. One finds similar pottery, since it was mold-produced;
one rarely finds weaving designs repeated. A collector of
modern art would not consider it out of line to place the
most abstract of modern designs beside those of the Peruvians; their ability to dissolve images into symmetrical and
geometric patterns, the stylization of subject matter, their
innate sense of transforming representational art in an over-
all decorative pattern, has been eulogized ever since this art
has been recognized as art.

16 Pottery and Pottery Makers

POTTERY is one of the oldest of skills in the Americas. The Indians did not have the potter's wheel (the whole idea of the wheel being completely absent in all forms). The ancient Peruvians, as all others in the Americas, used the coil method, and yet despite the primitive techniques this pottery is among the world's best, and its graceful forms rival the Greek vases of the best periods. Taken as a whole, the "arts" in these higher Peruvian civilizations are "fine arts in the best sense of this term." [2]

Inca pottery is well made, fine-grained, with a hardness almost metallic. Pottery shaping was made by first rolling clay into sausage form, then building spirally into the projected pot, one hand feeding the sausage-shaped core, the other pressing it into shape. This was then smoothed and molded by a small flat wooden disk; then it was dried, painted, and fired.

23. *A pottery brazier* (LEFT); *when placed in a room and filled with charcoal, this was capable of giving localized heat. A three-legged urn* (RIGHT) *was placed over a fire for cooking.*

Inca pottery has a wide range of shapes. There are the utilitarian, three-legged pots used by the warriors on campaign, the household pottery, strong and crude red, the enormous, beautifully shaped aryballus (although not like the Greek, from which its name derives)—a bottle-shaped pot with a pointed bottom, which fell to its side when emptied,

85

but was so exquisitely balanced that a jar, capable of holding
six to eight gallons of fermented *chicha*, could, when filled,
balance on that single point. The Inca aryballus had a long,
graceful neck and two band-shaped handles, used for holding a rope passed through them for carrying; it was the most
characteristic of Inca pottery. There were shallow dishes
for food, a type of service all seemed to have, and sometimes wonderfully decorated. There were beaker-shaped
vessels for drinking, and three-legged braziers, wide and
open-mouthed for heating the otherwise unheated rooms.

All, or almost all, of Inca pottery is a reflection of function; they made no contrast between art for its own sake and
art for a practical purpose. It is even misleading to speak
here of "art" in the aesthetic sense of today; the Incas, as
all other ancient peoples, were unaware of such distinctions.
Most of the world's ancient art was religious, except that of
the Mochicas, who had a secular "art." There is an intimate
relation in most of these societies between art and religion,
particularly in agrarian societies such as the Incas', where
art was bound up with religion for the purpose of humoring
the gods, cajoling them, or even compelling them by these ob-

24. *Inca pottery types. A tall, fragile ceremonial vase, unusual for the
utilitarian-minded Incas; polychrome eating plates (diameter about six
inches); (p. 87) varying forms of eating pots; a type, also found in wood,
for drinking corn* chicha.

jects to grant rain. All objects were made for use. There
was naturally, who could deny it, a real sense of beauty in
the craftsman. His absorption in geometrical ornamentation
must have come from his enjoyment of attractive lines and
forms, but everyone was a craftsman and leisure from the
fields, when it existed, was used for "thing" producing.

The designs of Inca pottery are very distinctive: usually

elaborate geometric patterns, so unalterably Inca they were
as identifiable as a Roman coin; for Inca pottery, as indeed
is equally true of other Peruvian pottery, is a diagnostic for
spatial relationships.

A history of preliterate people is mainly written in, and
determined by, the stylistic changes which can be seen in
their artifacts, and the artifact most sensitive to stylistic
change is pottery. An archaeologist seeking to understand
the time factor involved in a particular site makes a stratigraphical cut through a ruin; the potsherds that are found associated with other items of an Indian's life (worn clothing,
spindles, cordage, slings, bags, warheads, etc.) help to establish a typology of all other artifacts about them, included in
that time-space area. Through potsherds (design, shape, fir-
ing), the archaeologist can establish certain time subdivisons.
The knowledge derived from archaeology is more explicit
than literature or oft-told tales. Literary statements can be
challenged, but potsherds and artifacts are tangible and visi-
ble and reveal much. In the specific case of Inca pottery, it is
so distinct that wherever it is found—with other collaborat-
ing material—it marks the fact that the Incas were there.
"Virtually all of these [archaeological] techniques," wrote
the late Dr. Wendell Bennett, "depend heavily on ceramics,
since these are not only well preserved but also reflect styles."
Such a thing must have occurred to the first Persian ambassa-
dor sent to China, for when fingering a beautiful bowl he
said: "The date and the maker of the pot can be told by
the touch."

Pottery, too, can become language, as one sees among the
Mochicas. Their pottery is so realistically modeled that
every cultivated plant can be identified. The designs of their
garments, the dyes they used, the various social castes in
their society—rich man, poor man, beggerman, merchant,
chief—are found in their ceramics. Animals and birds are
there in profusion and so realistically done that it is almost
better than glyphic writing; for the maximum number of
mouth gestures is 144, but by rotating wrist, hand, and fingers, a man can produce 100,000 distinct elementary signs.

"The human hand is about twenty thousand times more versatile than the mouth." [31] This is reflected in the realistic Mochica pottery, which, with its wide range of subjects (even the sexual approach and attitudes are so many and varied that they promise a corpus of unplumbed sexual positions), constitutes a veritable plastic alphabet. [34]

While most were by necessity housebuilders or pottery makers or even weavers, there was, as in all complex societies, a class of specialists: some worked in gold, silver, wood; there were weavers of special fineness and specialized pottery makers—those living in regions of better clay. And as in all craft cultures, there was an excess; this was the lifeblood of trade. So while the Indian did not own his land nor the wool of the llamas which he herded, he was allowed his leisure time, and with this he created things in excess of his own consumption. He had no money, but he had value and he knew barter; out of this grew the market (as ancient as the Andes), which the Incas systematized into the *catu*.

17   The Market

MAN first knew peace through trade.

Throughout the prehistoric world, be it in the Americas or Africa or within that Fertile Crescent, hostilities were often suspended so that trade could be made. Trade, exchange, diffusion—through these activities man became more human. All the early routes of and for trade were luxury routes: "The extreme parts of the inhabited world," wrote Herodotus, "possess the most excellent products," and to these "extreme parts" men of all hues and colors passed in search of luxury products; the *Via Salaria*—the route to salt—was one of Rome's oldest roads. And in the Americas, one of the conquistadors, by following the route of the salt trays (a ceramic dish about the size of a bread pan) coming down from the interior of Colombia, traced that salt road and discovered the Chibchas, and with it the golden treasures of El Dorado.[73]

Man sought out amber from the earliest times, and the oldest road through Europe is the amber road over which man traveled from the Mediterranean to the Baltic to secure that wonderful fossilized soft rich pitch—that "special act of God." Other luxury items came over early pathways: *murex,* which yielded that Tyrian purple, silks, frankincense, and myrrh. So trade, when man became a city-dweller, was part of his urban revolution, perhaps not so much a revolution at all but the outgrowth of his gradual control of nature and the production of an excess of local products. It was just these concentrated surpluses that made possible the luxury tastes.

In addition to the amber routes, there were lapis lazuli routes, and silk roads; caravan cities such as Petra, Palmyra, Damascus, and many other famous caravansaries sprang up to meet the demand for luxury goods. So in the world search for luxury goods and transit, men often held roads under general amnesty; when men met for trade, hostilities were called off so that an exchange of products could take place. Markets, too, were the principal vehicles of diffusion—the essential dynamic factor in human progress. The market as a means of interchange of ideas and information gave the needed stimuli to human progress.

In preliterate America it was also luxury goods that stirred the Indian, although he was handicapped by geographical barriers and the lack of the "idea" of the wheel or draft animals. He was severely limited in his desire for luxuries (that "damned wantlessness" which Lenin complained of in the Russian peasant). But agricultural discoveries were exchanged rapidly through the medium of the trade market, so that within the entire Western Hemisphere almost every type of cultivated product was known throughout the three Americas. Obsidian for knives traveled thousands of miles from the place of origin; emeralds, which were found only in the narrow corner of a mountain called Muzo in Colombia, found their way to Mexico and south into Peru as luxury items. The Mexican markets brimmed with luxury items: chocolate, vanilla, gold and silver objects, feather weavings, ornamented sandals. And thus, the Peruvian.

Markets under the Inca Empire were frequent and general, but trade was purely local and commerce a government monopoly. The need for markets within the empire was an important element in the economic structure of the realm. "In order," wrote Garcilaso de la Vega, "that labor might not be so continuous as to become oppressive, the Inca ordained that there should be three holidays every month in which the people should divert themselves with various games. He also commanded that there should be three fairs every month, when the laborers in the field should come to the market and hear anything that the Inca or his council might have ordained." They called these markets *catus*.

This system of using the market as an official decree-dispensing method is remembered in one of the smaller market centers of Cuzco itself; it is known as Rimacpampa, the "Speaking Place," where the people gathered to hear the Inca equivalent of "Hear ye, hear ye. . . ."

The orbit of the people was limited; fairs were mostly local, and an Indian used the royal roads only with the consent of the local chieftain. In many of the large Inca cities (and still to be seen on the fragments of the Inca road that winds its way through the Andes) are the posts, the halting places, where guards made certain of who used the road and for what purpose. Tolls were set up at all the large bridges for travelers to markets, as was recorded by the first European observation. On January 14, 1533, when Hernando Pizarro made the journey to the coast to hurry up the flow of gold which was to ransom the captured Inca, they came to the Andean village of Piga along the royal road which there crossed the Santa River which was "spanned by two bridges close together made of network . . . By one of these bridges the common people cross over and a porter is stationed there to receive transit dues. . . ." [17]

The economic interdependence of the various provinces did not require complex trade, and so the markets were not warranted alone by economic necessity; the stuff and products wanted were luxury goods, mostly interchange between the mountain and coastal people on one side and the mountain people and the jungle people on the other.

What was luxury to the Indian? From the coast came cotton—soft and different, easy to weave, and although not as warm as alpaca wool, yet luxury; all classes of society sought it and the Spanish on their arrival found the public storehouses full of it. There was a different set of dyeing colors—always important to the weaver—and many types of rock mordants from the coast that gave cotton subtle hues; there was *achiote,* which rendered a carmine color, and purple from seashells. Among the foods there were seaweed (still beloved by the Indian and still to be seen in their markets), seashell food (the great shell conchas were used as trumpets), dried fish of every description, reeds for basketmaking, and many forms of hotland food products. The jungle people brought feathers for the feather mosaic weavings, *chonta-palm* (an iron-hard wood) much used by the Incas; there were birds, jungle game, and batwings' fur (from which a silklike cloth was made for the Inca), dyestuffs, and many Homeric simples such as quinine, ipecac, sassafras, *guayusa* (used for a febrifuge), rubber, and gum latex from the sapodilla tree, strong tobacco leaf, and narcotics.

The Andean people brought to this type of market their excess manufactures: weavings, bowls, carvings, potatoes, *chuñu,* corn—that which they did not themselves consume; and since the empire levied no property taxes, only *mita* labor service, they were free to exchange any accumulated movable property.

There was, as aforementioned, no money, "that great human convenience" says Madge Jenison in her stimulating book on *Roads,* "by which a symbol of life is simplified." Without coinage the monetary principle was barter. Nor did the regime intervene in the spirited exchange at the markets. "No value," says Garcilaso de la Vega, "nor standard was fixed in these exchanges by any public authority, for this was left wholly to the satisfaction of the bargaining parties." Although the Incas, as the rest of the native Americans, were out of the stream of Old World culture that brought in its current the wheel, the horse, coinage, and writing, they were forming, none the less, a society similar to the early Egyptian and Sumerian civilizations. They were already part of the urban revolution that changed man from a food-gatherer to a food-grower, part of the settled community that produced the city-state and class society.

In ancient Sumer the land was also communally held: "owned by a god who stood for the community which formed his people . . . but it was parcelled out among god's people —the citizens—to be worked as individual allotments . . . The surplus accumulated," writes V. Gordon Childe, "was deposited in the Sumerian temples and made it worth-while to organize caravans." [13] The Inca system was somewhat similar except that there was no such thing as a merchant class in this empire, in fact no merchant at all. Yet, as everywhere, the stomach was the guiding impulse, and markets and trade, no matter how different the society nor how far removed, followed the pattern that was man's.

Pedro de Cieza de León, that most accurate of observers, tells something about them in 1549, long after the departure of Inca glory. The barbaric pageantry that went with these markets can only be dimly surmised: "In all parts of this kingdom of Peru we who have travelled over it know that there are great fairs or markets, where the natives make their bargains. Among those the greatest and richest was formerly in the city of Cuzco, for even in the time of the Spaniards its greatness was caused by the gold which was bought and sold there and by the other things of all kinds that were sent into the city. But this market or fair at Cuzco did not equal the superb one at Potosí, where the traffic was so great that among the Indians alone, without including Christians, twenty-five or thirty thousand golden pesos exchanged hands daily. This is wonderful, and I believe that no fair in the world can be compared to it. . . ."

18 Holidays and Games — Dance and Music

THE HOLIDAYS, which were public ceremonials, were many and elaborate, bound to the markets and to the ceremonial year which was tied up with the agricultural year.

The Inca year was divided into twelve months, each month named after its ceremony. The year began in December with *Capac Raymi*, the "magnificent festival" month. There were many sports and games attached to the festivals, and the coming-of-age rites were held, with the boys of the upper class receiving the breechclout. There was the month of the "small ripening" and the "great ripening"; there were others which were called the month of the "dance of the young maize," and later the "festival of the water"; a complete list as given by Dr. Luis Valcárcel [66] appears here:

GREGORIAN MONTHS	PERUVIAN MONTHS*	TRANSLATION
December	Capac Raimi	Magnificent festival
January	Huchuy Pocoy	Small ripening
February	Hatun Pocoy	Great ripening
March	Paucar Warai	Garment of flowers
April	Airiway	Dance of young maize
May	Aimuari	Song of the harvest
June	Inti Raimi	Festival of the sun
July	Anta Situwa	Earthly purification
August	Capac Situwa	General purification—sacrifice
September	Coya Raimi	Festival of the queen
October	Uma Raimi	Festival of the water
November	Ayamarca	Procession of the dead

Although these were observed throughout the empire and reenacted wherever there were great Sun temples, Cuzco, as Rome, was the focus of most of the important events; here they were the most elaborate. The stirring pomp and meticulous ritual connected with all of the festivals has not been exaggerated by the first Spaniards; they are fully documented in the remains of the gaudy garments that were worn

* Spellings have been modified to conform with the usage of Quechua words in this book.

by the participants which have been recovered from the
tombs.

The ritual attending was naturally part of the whole trance
of being; the mimetic dances and songs, movements and
voices, were all part of the elaboration given to the earth
mysteries by the priests of the Sun. It was precisely the
color format needed by the Indian, who was, by the nature
of his environment, hemmed in and dulled by the narrow
corner of his world. Inca festivals gave ordinary man a
sense of belonging; this collective hypnotism, these ecstatic
states of ecstasy robbed him of his self-possession, and to
paraphrase a French anthropologist,[36] "transported him to
a life beyond life," and gave him the feeling that the particular plea to the gods, at the moment, had been attained. And
it provided him later, in the long, dark hours in his mountain
house, with the subject for talk to fill in the interstices of
extended night.

Holidays might last for a day or for a week. There might
be public dancing, such as when hundreds of radiantly clothed
Chosen Women danced with Huáscar's Chain. There could
be games and sports. There was always drinking, for the
Indian was expected to get drunk, which he did, quaffing
immense quantities of fermented *chicha;* ritual drunkenness
was as essential to a good festival as agricultural discipline
was to a good harvest.

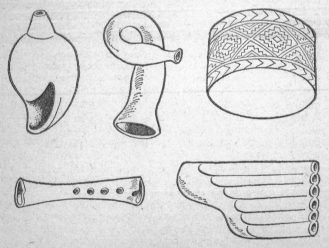

25. *Types of Inca musical instruments.*
Conch-shell horn *(potóto);* Bone flute *(piroro);* Tambourine *(tin-ya);*
Reed flute *(quena);* Reed-made Panpipes *(antara).*

Games at the festivals differed from those played by the Indian boy (which consisted mainly of spinning a top by whipping, a sort of "pile-on" game with potatoes, flipping small counters against the wall—called "lagging" in the United States—and a game called "Puma" which was something like Run, Sheep, Run). Sports at fair days were Olympic: there were foot races, such as described by Padre Acosta, during the "magnificent" month, when "young sons of the nobility used to race one another up Huanacauri hill"; there were mock battles in which village would be pitted against village, or group against group in a large square arranged for the purpose; there was the sport of throwing the bola (similar to roping steers), where the young man watched the practiced hand quickly enmesh a running llama by a skillful toss of the lariat ingeniously balanced by three stones or metal balls, which entwined the animal in a moment as the snakes ententacled Laocoön.

There were other variants in the games. In the month of December, on the day fixed for the feast, men and girls came to a predetermined place among the fruit gardens, whose ripening they were to celebrate. Men and women were completely naked. At a given signal they started off in a race, upon which bets were placed, toward some hill at a distance. Each man who overtook any woman in the race "enjoyed her on the spot."

The musical instruments of the Incas were as limited as the variation of their dance. By their nature they were self-limiting; they were mostly percussion and wind instruments, and strictly bucolic. Drums were made of a hollow log and covered either with llama or tapir hide (they varied from small drums used by women to war drums used by warriors). Whatever the variety, they were beaten by a rubber-knobbed stick, and their drumming had nothing of the quality of the sensuous music of the Mediterranean world. A tambourine (*tin-ya*) was used in dances. There were copper and silver *chanrara* bells, attached to clothes and hung on bracelets and dangling from wooden maces. On the dancers' legs were attached anklets of silver bells or shells, and snail-shell (*churu*) rattles.

The most stirring of the trumpets was the *potóto*, made from an enormous seashell; it is monotonic, but the effects of a massed chorus of these in war ritual must have been stirring. The Incas seem not to have had, or at least did not use, the large trumpets known to the coastal people, which have been found both in metal and ceramic forms.

Flutes were many and varied; the flute, *quena*, made like a recorder, ranged from two to six notes. There were flutes made from the femurs of jaguars and human beings (*piroros*), but the most typical was the syrinx or Panpipes of cane or pottery made in a minor scale. This *antara* is still found throughout the Andes.

There have been few studies of Andean music. The music was strange to the ears of the conquistadors. It was anathema to the padres, who feared its pagan overtones so that they scarcely mention it; and the d'Harcourts, who made a collection of "Inca" music, the type of which is still heard throughout the Peruvian Andes and now obtainable in records, used uncontrolled sources so that it may be said with considerable conviction that we know little about Inca music, and that "detailed studies of native music are urgently needed. Time is fast running out for this sort of survival, and will soon eclipse all memory of it." [25]

Music was bound up with the dance and the dance with religion; all forms of religious expression involved dancing.[32] The dance (*taki*) itself included singing; it was part of the collective hypnotism. The songs were repeated endlessly, monotonously; the evolutions of the dancer, the ornaments, and the furiously rapid movements robbed all of the onlookers of their self-possession and gave them a feeling that their needs —for which the dance was designed—had been supplied. Masks and costumes were important in these dances, and they have survived to a surprising degree among the Andean Indians of the present day. There were dresses in mimicry of animals (and the dancers were always accoutered in the pelt of the animal depicted); there were victory dances (*cachuas*) limited to warriors who, holding hands and in full military panoply, formed a great circle, moving and writhing as a snake. The drumbeat for this was usually performed on what had been the body of an enemy: the skin of the whole body of a dead man had been flayed and the belly stretched to form a drum; the whole body acted as a sound box, throbbings coming out of the open mouth—grotesque but effective. Such dances, widespread throughout Peru, can be seen illustrated on the pottery of the famed pre-Inca culture of the Mochicas.

There was a farm dance (*hayl-yi*) of the common people; here the Indian farmers carried the instruments of their work, and they moved through the dance in mimicry of tilling the fields; such a dance is still seen in the Andes today. Those who watched the dance and those who acted in it had in common the mystical communion, the fusion of the participants with the particular god which they were attempting to pacify.

The most elaborate was the *way-yaya*, the formal dance

of the Inca family, not much different in idea and substance from the dance of that other Sun King, Louis XIV, which opened the minuet. It was performed very solemnly and in a stately manner, self-limiting and self-sufficing, two steps forward, one step backward, as the line of dancers moved slowly toward the golden stool on which sat the Lord-Inca.

African dances are sensual, Arabian, erotic, but the dances of the Andean Indians possess a monotony that, if watched long enough, can make one howl. It is so now—and might well have been then—yet it must have been a very wonderful thing to see, and how one wishes at this moment to turn back time's clock to see all this Tawantinsuyu, "Land of the Four Directions," dancing beneath the Andean sun.

Still the picture of the life of these people as one long joyous idyll cadenced by dance and the hypnotic beat of the tom-tom has been terribly overdrawn. Distance, of course, has lent this barbaric empire enchantment; it was hardly that. From birth to death—and even beyond—their lives were saturated with the supernatural: their entire preoccupation was with the "unseen powers"; they were magicbound every moment of their lives. Although in this Inca welfare state, man moved as close to Utopia as he ever would in the Andean world, judged by any other standard it was still a hard and monotonous existence.

The Rousseau idyll that men are born good and happy and that society has made them wicked was simply a dialectic artifice, yet it has set the tone of the literature on the American Indian. It seems that, no matter how scientific the approach to the subject of the Incas, they still retain this romantic tinge.

Since then the theme of the Noble Savage has pursued us. When Jean Jacques Rousseau told women to copy nature and "nurse your children," a confused palingenesis of Madonnas took place; queens posed as shepherdesses, diplomats became natural philosophers, legislators proclaimed the natural rights of man—and the people, naturally "good" of course, took the bait and cut so many thousands of human heads that the sewers of Paris gagged on the viscous streams of blood. Fontenelle long ago observed, "All men are much alike so that there are no people whose foibles should make us tremble." The Incas were people—that is, they were good and bad, warlike and pacific, aggressive, cruel, revengeful, suspicious, libidinous, and generous. They lived out their lives within this human framework. To indulge in an idyllic representation of their society contradicts itself. To judge them by our form of history is equally illogical; history is *a priori* amoral. "Nature," as Remy de Gourmont wrote, "ignores the adjectives of 'good' and 'bad'; they are illusions, put up from time to time in a form of ironical antithesis or even in ignorance to explain away human actions." The flow that separates civilized man from uncivilized man is a rivulet that any child can, and does, step over.

19 Crime and Punishment

THE INCA EMPIRE was a functioning theocracy: the Inca was god and man, and any crime was at once disobedience and sacrilege.

The people of the Inca formed a very simple and sensible notion of evil—their functions and natural feelings were tied up with their prejudices. The moral base of Inca society was founded on ancient mores which had, since eternal time, ruled man in the Americas. Parental authority was strict, in fact severe. Parents had the respect of their children, and the daily round of the child and its education was by doing; a child had practically no life apart from his parents. In our society, in contrast, lives of parents and children are divided; there is the child's world of fantasy and reality, amusement and literature in which the parents enter albeit briefly and then almost as penitents. "Don't touch," "don't use," "don't drink," are the prime moral forces urged upon children, and the insistence on *meum et teum*, mine and thine, must be taught, enforced, disciplined. None of this existed in the Inca Empire; learning was by doing; education and "becoming-of-age" were by mimicry and seeing; there was no strong contrasting line of conduct between child and adult. Out of this continuity of parent and child grew the mores which formed the base of the Incas' justice, and out of it came a simple code of existence—and even this existed thousands of years before the Incas' advent.

Murder, violence, theft, lying, adultery, and laziness were, since they are human, motivations present in Inca society; all were punishable. Murder was punished by death: hanging, stoning, or merely pushing over a cliff was the method (there are several such execution places known, notably at the site of Ollantaytambo, near to Cuzco). Punishment, however, was mitigated if murder was done in self-defense or in a rage against an adulterous wife. Stealing carried with it its own prognosis—death. Since one pilfered from a god, taking anything from public property was the most heinous of crimes: breaking into the Inca's storage chambers, destroying bridges, and entering the precincts of the Chosen Women. Stealing was especially peccant since there was virtually no want and so there would normally be no temptation to steal.

There was no incentive for the common Indian to accumulate possessions.

The basic honesty of the Indian under Inca rule is attested not alone by learned Spanish judges but by one of the conquistadors, the famous Mancio Sierra de Leguisamo, the one "who gambled away the sun." * In the preamble to his will, filed in Cuzco, he wrote: "The Incas governed in such a way that there was not a thief, not a criminal, not an idle man . . . the Indians left the doors of their houses open, a stick crosswise in front of the door was a sign that the owner was not in . . . and nobody would enter."

Theft was regarded as an aberration, and when theft did occur (the machinery of justice was administered merely by accused and accusers telling their sides of the story to a *curaca*) there was a differentiation between robbery from malice and robbery through necessity; if the Indian did so through want, the official was punished for his lack of administration which brought about the crime.

Since laziness deprived the Inca of the Indian's services, this was punished first by public rebuke, then stoning, and, if continued, by liquidation. (A counterpart in our own country: one may murder and escape the consequences, but nonpayment of taxes brings inescapable punishment.)

Drunkenness was allowed, and was condemned only when occurring at the wrong time, i.e., when the Indian was supposed to be working; then drunkenness was a crime, since it encouraged laziness.

Conservation of animals, too, was in the Inca code of justice. The punishment for the unauthorized killing of a female llama, or the killing of a female vicuña when not part of a royal hunt, was death; as aristocrats everywhere regard it, poaching ranked as one of the cardinal crimes.

The administration of justice was *hiwaya;* in addition to the death penalty, which was usually rapid, ruthless, and impartial, there were other forms of punishment: exile to mines, a term spent in the moist jungles of the Montaña or on the coca plantations, or other forms of public rebuke, which, it was held, were almost as bad as death itself.

"For the Incas," said Garcilaso de la Vega, "never made laws to frighten their vassals, but always with the intention of enforcing them on those who ventured to transgress them. . . ."

---

* This conquistador received as his part of the Inca's golden hoard of Cuzco a huge golden image of the Sun. As soon as he had it, he, with the other soldiers, began to gamble throughout the night. In the process he lost it—from which rose the proverb "To play away the sun before the dawn."

There were, it appears, two forms of justice: Inca law distinguished crimes involving nobles from those concerning the common people (a concept dramatized by George Orwell in his *Animal Farm* wherein people are equal but some people are more equal than others). But here, under the Inca system, the people of the upper classes were given more severe punishments for infractions than the lower. What was mere public rebuke for the common people became for the noble, when involved, banishment; what was torture for the common Indian, such as having one of his eyes torn out, for the noble was—death.

The Incas codified and systematized the moral code of the Andean people, and since these codes of conduct were based on the collective conscience of the *ayllu,* therein lay its strength.

20 Medicine, Magic, and Curing

THE ANDEAN PEOPLE (and that is to say, everyone in preliterate South America) was from birth to death tied to the supernatural; disease was superphysical, and as such had to be cured with both medicine and magic. If a harvest failed or an Indian fell ill from no apparently sufficient cause, this proceeded obviously from witchcraft, or perhaps the afflicted had somehow offended the unseen powers. The supernatural had made an intrusion into this life; magic and medicine were inextricably bound together.

There are no connected studies of Inca medicine, even though Peruvian botanists have identified numerous plants used by the Inca shaman; there were many plants, doubtless, that were efficacious in curing, but no matter what the disease it was bound up with magic.

Magic is the arrest of the intelligence, and while the "doctor" as well as the patient was aware of the connection between the related phenomena of illness and medicine, their minds were only slightly sensitive to the contradictions. "Magic," wrote Raoul Allier, "is a dream destined to act as a counterpoise to a state of unrest, an awakening dream obedient to rules, fantastic, indeed, but so methodical as at times to appear scientific."

When an Indian fell ill, a *hampi-camayoc*, literally a "remedy keeper," was called in. The usual beginning, after a display of the shaman's kit, was either a fast, a salt emetic, or a purgative root. Later, after a routine of enchantments, the *hampi-camayoc* acted as a masseur, rubbing the patient until he extracted by sleight of hand some foreign substance: a needle, a pin, a pebble. He had removed the "cause." After this, medicine was prescribed. This was not a fraud or chicanery. Patient and curer shared the illusion that was created; they both knew that the disease was caused by something lodged in the body, but to effect a final and permanent cure was something else. The "wild" Indians of the Upper Amazon used a brew made from a vine, *aya-huasca*—the vine of the souls—which both patient and medicine man drank; out of the visions brought on by this powerful alkaloid, "instructions" as to the cause and cure were given. Purging and bleeding were common medical

102

practices among them; these techniques, it will be recalled, were also common medical practices in the Western world up to 1800.

The Indians had a wide knowledge of drug plants. Many have entered our own pharmacopoeia, such as quinine, cocaine (from the coca plant), ipecac (used as an emetic), belladonna (which yields a mild narcotic anodyne)—the list could be extended. The Inca medical practitioners had tobacco (*sayri*)—used as snuff to clear the nasal passages—the juice of the *matec-llu* (a water plant for the eyes), the resin of the *mulli* tree to help heal wounds, and so on to a very impressive number of plants which had real, not alone magical, power to effect cures. Yet despite the very *real* quality of the drug, the patient never escaped the power of magic; this application of magic, in the last analysis, was the final resort, needed to pass from illness (*oñ-qoy*) into the state of being *kamasqa*, i.e., cured.

It was socially profitable to be a "remedy keeper"; a good one or fortunate one could acquire new tunics, gold and silver ornaments as payment. But it was also dangerous. Since illness was caused by bewitchment, the medicine man could be, and often was, held accountable if the patient died; he was in fact held by the family to be the murderer. On the coast, the Mochicas would bury the patient tied to the trussed-up "doctor" and expose him to death in the desert.

What diseases afflicted the Indian? Again, this interesting ground has not been consistently explored. Of a certainty white man brought all the civilized diseases to the indigenous American; the introduction of smallpox, tuberculosis, measles, and mumps wrecked havoc upon the Indian. In turn, the American gave white man that best-known civilized disease—syphilis. Yellow fever and malaria presumably were present; they are tropicopolitan. Most of the lung diseases—pneumonia, bronchitis, and the common cold—were apparently present; infant mortality from this type of disease was, and still is, high. There were other endemic diseases which left dreadful marks. *Uta* is a destructive ulcerative disease, which begins about the nose, and the disease eats away the nose cartilage and the lips, leaving the face horribly mutilated; it appears pictured frequently on Mochica pottery, where, incidentally, all of the native indigenous diseases are depicted. It was called, in Quechua, *acapana ayapcha*, which merely means "red-fringed clouds," a reference to the bleeding red walls of the face ulcer. *Verruga* was another very feared disease; it occurs usually in valleys with an altitude of about 6,000 feet, and is transmitted by an insect (*titira*). It first manifests itself by a sore throat, pain in the bones,

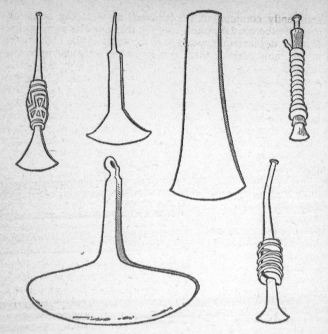

26. *Inca and pre-Inca surgical instruments. These were found in graves with gauze bandages and a form of tourniquet which was primitive but very effective.*
Scalpel; Bronze *tumi* for making incisions in bone; Larger bronze scalpel; Bronze scalpel with wooden handle; *Tumi;* Bronze scalpel.

and then an eruption of red-colored pimples which increase in magnitude to the size of suppurating volcanoes. There is high fever and the warty, corrugated excrescences bleed until the sufferer is exhausted and dies from anemia. The disease is endemic. In 1869 it broke out so virulently that for months it stopped the building of the Peruvian railways. The natives treated it with an infusion of roots called *huayra-huayra.*

On the coast there were other subcutaneous diseases, one of which covered the arms, legs, and face with large pustules and, if an Indian survived it, left his body marked with indelible spots. This disease, immortalized by the Mochicas in their pottery, shows an Indian pocked with marks that have been mistaken by some archaeologists for smallpox.

There were other native and endemic diseases. Cretinism —physical deformity and degeneracy—appeared and was sufficiently common to be depicted, as were the other diseases, in the coastal pottery, among them *mal de pott*, another form of degeneracy appearing in the face. In the high Andes, in the snow regions, there was *surumpi*, a violent inflammation of the eyelids caused by looking at the dazzling light— a snow blindness—but which here was so acute that the eyes swelled and bled and if it was uncared for resulted in total blindness. Altitude sickness, *soroche*, affected all who ventured into the high altitudes without proper acclimatization. By studying the various diseases so accurately displayed on Mochica pottery, a physician trained in tropical medicine could obtain a very good idea of endemic diseases prevalent in pre-Hispanic America.

But this much is certain: like the cultivated plants of America, so with the American diseases; few are identical between the Old World and the New, with the exception of tropicopolitan yellow fever and malaria. Both of these facts are immutable evidence that there was no continuous contact between the two worlds until white men broke the cultural barrier in the year 1492.

Surgery, anesthetics, and other operative practices were considerably advanced in Peru. A blow on the head, a kick in the rump, a severed leg took the native out of the realm of metaphysics and brought him to earth to seek a rational explanation of the pathological processes. The Peruvians, i.e., many of the cultures which preceded the Incas and the Incas themselves, performed the most delicate operations on the skull, trepanning heads of warriors wounded by a blow from a battle-ax and removing the pieces of skull that pressed on the brain and caused paralysis. Many patients, of course, died (as they do even now under such operations), but many lived, as is evidenced by the enormous number of skulls found in graves with the bone tissue renewed, showing the success of the operation.

Although the Incas seemed to have brought this type of surgery to perfection (they had to, since they were engaged in far-flung conquests involving much war), the technique of trepanning skulls was known two thousand years before them, for trepanned skulls are found in the graves of various pre-Inca cultures. Although there has been interest in trepanned skulls, and the techniques and speculations about them have appeared in literature for more than a century, it was not until two Peruvian surgeons, Francisco Graña and Esteban Rocca, undertook a serious study of ancient Peruvian surgical techniques that this interesting phase of Peruvian cultural development was fully appreciated. Now this profound study places the ancient Peruvians in an even higher category of advancement.

One of the most common of military weapons was the *macana,* a weapon whose "business end" was rounded or star-shaped, cut in either heavy stone or cast in bronze. The best place of attack was the head, and the greatest number of casualties in battle were skull injuries. Sometime in their early history, the Peruvian Indians somehow raveled out the connection between the wound inflicted by the *macana* and pressure on the brain; out of this observation arose the technique of skull trepanning. Over ten thousand of such trepanned skulls have been found in graves throughout Peru, and in many tombs surgical instruments have been found: obsidian arrowheads shaped for trepanning, bronze *tumi* knives for cutting, scalpels, pincers, needles for sutures—in short, instruments which can be compared favorably with those known to the Romans. With these instruments Drs. Graña and Rocca actually performed trepanations of the skull on a living patient, using Inca operative techniques (except, of course, with a general anesthetic). They used the Inca form of tourniquet (applied about the whole of the round of the head), and proved the efficacy of the ancient operative techniques. The Indians had forms of gauze and cotton swabs, used a tourniquet, perfected local and perhaps general anesthesia. In addition to skull trepanning, many other forms of amputations were performed (archaeological evidence exists on Mochica pottery). In short, pre-Inca and Inca medicine and surgical practice seem to have been just as advanced, perhaps in many respects more so, than when the gifted Ambroise Paré of France was taking medicine out of its medieval doldrums in sixteenth-century Europe.

Little or nothing is known of the use of anesthetics and narcotics among Peruvians; about all that can be deduced is the types of narcotics that were available to them. Belladonna (*Datura ferox*) is well known; it yields atropine, and was once widely used as "twilight sleep" for childbirth. *Aya-huasca* ("vine of the souls"), a narcotic malpighiad (*Bani-steria caapi*), grows in the Montaña on the lower slopes which lead to the Upper Amazon. The roots yield three forms of alkaloids, which were found to contain "a very active material producing effects on the central nervous system." [75] The *wil-ka* tree (identified botanically as *Piptadenia colubrina* and related to the acacias) produced a seed which, after being roasted and brayed, was used as a snuff. Little is known of it, although such Inca cities as Vilcapampa (i.e., *wil-ka*), and Vilcas-huamán, tell of the tree's presence and its presumed importance. It was a narcotic; whether it produced visions or anesthesia or was used as an emetic is not known.

Finally in the list of possible anesthetics is the well-known coca or *cuca,* which yields cocaine; there is no doubt about its efficacy as a narcotic. None of those aforementioned would seem, at least from here, to have been able to produce the general anesthesia which would be needed to prepare a patient with a battered skull to receive the assaults of a native "surgeon." In that case he would merely have to suffer through it as did Samuel Pepys when, without anesthesia, he had the "stones" removed from his gall bladder on March 26, 1658, "since it pleased God that I was cut of the stone at Mrs. Turner's in Salisbury Court." One just lay back and took it until merciful narcosis short-circuited the whole nervous system into temporary oblivion.

Coca, its use and disuse, has been a subject of debate—now more than ever—since white men came upon it in full use among the Incas. Coca is as old as Peru; of it Pedro de Cieza de León wrote: "If coca did not exist—neither would Peru." And not alone in Peru, but throughout all the Andes and into the Amazon; today there are over five million people addicted to it.

Coca (botanically it is *Erythroxylum coca*) is cultivated in the warm *yungas* and on the slopes of the eastern Andes. It is a low, thick bush, with glossy leaves not unlike tea leaves. The leaves are picked four times within fourteen months, very carefully sun-dried, then later shade-dried, so that the green of the leaf is retained. This leaf contains an alkaloid (chemically methyl-benzyl-ecogine) and has entered medicine as cocaine. It was once widely used for a local anesthetic, and up until 1900 was thought to be a wonderful nerve tonic. Coca wine was widely drunk until the Pure Foods and Drug Act prevented it. Sigmund Freud was an inveterate user of it.

Garcilaso "the Inca" wrote, "*Cuca* is a shrub the height and thickness of the vine; it has a few branches and on them many delicate leaves the width of the thumb and in length about half the length of the thumb—and of agreeable odor but not very sweet . . . so pleasant is *cuca* to the Indians that they prefer it to gold and silver and precious stones. . . . They chew them but do not swallow, they merely savour the fragrance and swallow the juice. *Cuca,*" Garcilaso goes on, "preserves the body from many infirmities and our doctors [i.e., doctors in Spain] use it in powder form to arrest and placate the swelling of wounds. . . ." Coca was, as almost everything in Peru, pre-Inca; its presence is indicated by finding it in tombs and graves reaching far back into time in precisely the same form as it was used in the times of the Incas and is used today, small woolen bags were filled with coca leaves, and with them a small gourd holding the lime —lime which was made by burning seashells or limestone. Now as then, the method is to make a wad of coca leaves about the size of a brazil nut. The quid is stuffed into the side of the mouth, into which is placed a pinch of the lime, which helps to extract the juice. This when swallowed makes the chewer less susceptible to cold, thirst, hunger, and fatigue.

The Incas called it the "divine plant," and, as they did with all they touched, they extended and regulated the system of its agriculture. The plantations were vastly extended under Inca rule. Harvesting occurred three to four times a year, and the leaves were plucked when ripe, just before falling. The crop of leaves (*matu*) was kept covered overnight in a shed (*matuhuasi*), and sun-dried the following day. Drying was a delicate process. The vocabulary which grew up about the planting, harvesting, packing, and shipping shows to what extent the process entered the Inca world.

Mastication of the coca is called *coquer*, a word now half-Spanish, half-Quechua. The masticated leaves form a ball (*hacchu*), to which is added the lime-ash (*llucta*). Archaeologists are not agreed on the extent to which coca-chewing was general among the Incas. It was limited, it is believed, to the nobles and the soothsayers, i.e., the *amautas*, and to the *chasquis*, or couriers, who were forced to go at high speeds in high altitudes—and to the very old. Indubitably it was fully regulated, as was everything else in the Inca Empire. However, on the arrival of the Spaniards, with the Inca governing system thrown into complete chaos, the common Indians, the official restrictions lifted, turned whole-sale to the use of the narcotic coca. The Spaniards enlarged the coca plantations; they controlled its sale (it *still* is a state monopoly under republican Peru), and within a few years many waxed rich upon it. As Pedro de Cieza de León avers: "There are some persons in Spain who are rich from the produce of this *cuca* [he was writing in 1550], having traded with it, sold and re-sold it in the Indian markets." And just as the pagan religion, the Sun, drew some of its susten-ance from coca, so then did the church of the conquerors of the land. "It hath too yet another great profit, and this that the greater portion of the income of the bishop and canons and other clergy of the Cathedral Church of Cuzco derives *tithes* upon the *cuca* leaves."

What precisely the coca does to the human body is no longer in doubt: if one reads the evidence, it is there to see.[24] There is, among those long addicted to coca-chewing, a high frequency in the degeneration of sensory reception, disturbances of eyes, enlarged thyroid, and general physical breakdown; a list of the moral and physical breakdowns caused by this addiction is terrifying. Coca may well sustain the Indian at these high altitudes, but eventually it leaves him an addict, apathetic, abulic, and stupid. Although the Incas had it and used it primarily for religious ends, it had its uses among elders or *amautas*, and was also used for divination, when it was burned as frankincense (the sacred fumigant, which warded off ill-fortune or pacified the earth goddess).

21 Death and the Little Gods

No MATTER how organized the state—and here everything, as has been aforesaid, was prescribed from birth— nothing could prevent death, the final chapter of life. And with this there was much preoccupation. Death did not conform, it was unlike anything else, so when it came, as it had to come to all Indians, it imposed a strain on the living. The Indians were careful never to anger the undead, the recently dead. For the dead were in reality living, only they had become invisible, impalpable, and—for the discomfort of the living—invulnerable; hence the great preoccupation with the comforts for the dead.

"Indeed," said Pedro de Cieza de León, speaking of the immense monuments that surrounded Ayaviri, hard upon Lake Titicaca, "the place is . . . worthy of note, especially the great tombs, which are so numerous that they occupy more space than the habitations of the living. . . ."

Even death divided the common man from the higher. Death merely continued the dichotomy: the *puric* died almost as he had lived, communally; only for the great were reserved the enormous prestige burials. There has been described the ordinary Indian's way of life, his appearance, dress, language, marriage customs, birth, his round of daily life, his arts and crafts, his markets and his holidays, and the division between the worker and the Lord-Inca was sharply marked in all of these. Clothing (among the lower class) was worn until it became too old to retain; tunics of the Lord-Inca were never worn twice. The Indian had one wife; the Inca had hundreds. The taxpayer had few privileges, the Inca created them. The Inca had considerable education; the Indian found his through the empiricism of his life.

In death, the little man had to be content with the little gods. His end, like his beginning, was a simple ritual. Although he had many gods, only one, the creator-god Tici Viracocha, was very real; Pachacamac led a pantheon of lesser gods, and these gods, like those of the older world, had special functions and powers. The Indian believed in immortality; in fact he believed one never died, for when shrived and flexed, the dead body merely became undead and it took on the influences of the unseen powers.

110

The *ayllu* was maimed by death; it undermined the clan, which was a mutual-aid society. At death, the survivors put on a sort of mourning. Women lopped off their long hair, shrouded their faces, and offered food to all who came to the rites. There was a slow dance performed near the body; the women beat on small drums and sang dirges. The body of the dead one was flexed, knees up to chin, and shrouded in his own tunic and wrapped in cloth. In the Andes his tomb was under rock eaves; the small catacombs—round, square, or oval—were made of field stone and cemented with adobe mud. Inside the tomb, the sitting body had placed about it food, bowls of *chicha*, and the many small things of his life —if a warrior, the instruments of his trade; if a weaver of note, those artifacts. A woman was given her loom, her color boxes, and wool to spin. All of this was of supreme importance, for the dead did not wish to go. They were hostile to the living, and they had to be made comfortable so that in their loneliness they would not carry off the living to comfort them. Death was contagious.

The dead now became *huaca*, i.e., godlike and mysterious; they exercised a charm so that one had to be careful that none of the *ayllu* offended the dead. The dead were numbered now among the unseen powers and had to be propitiated. Yet in time the dead died, and gradually, unless they were such as the Inca-God (who, even when dead, was surrounded by gaudy ritual), were forgotten. The ordinary Indian became absorbed in the trouble of living and one can speculate on the existence of his skepticism about the undead. Elsewhere, for example in the necropolis of ancient Myrina in Aeolis (now in Turkey), people buried the dead as the Incas did, with the things of their lives. They knew that the dead were hard to please, but they also knew that they would *never* come back. They encircled the dead with diadems of gold, but so thin that a breath would reduce them to powder. They regulated their accounts with the dead as cheaply as possible; the obolus they put into the mouths of the dead to pay Charon to cross the river Styx was only a poor brass coin.

Yet the hold of religion on the Indian was enormous and very real, for life was practical and religion was life, and since all life was controlled by the all-pervading unseen powers, the Indian had to come to a tacit agreement with them for his own well-being. This, then, was the life of the Indian—typical of the unknown number who formed the base of the pyramid which was the Inca realm. At the summit was the Inca.

"At the base of the pyramid was the *puric*, an able-bodied male worker. Ten workers were controlled by a straw boss;

ten straw bosses had a foreman; ten foreman in turn had a supervisor . . . The hierarchy continued in this fashion to the chief of a tribe, reportedly composed of ten thousand workers, to the governor of a province, to the ruler of one of the four quarters of the Inca empire, and finally to the emperor, the Sapa Inca . . ." [8]

1. The Sun Temple, Vilcas-huamán, 200 miles northwest of Cuzco. Composed of three tiers, a stone gate, and thirty-three stone steps (see plan, Figure 37), it is the only surviving sun temple in the Inca Empire. *Victor W. von Hagen*

2. Detail of a doorway of the fortress of Sacashuamán. As the massive stones had to fit perfectly, the architectural features had to be worked out well in advance of construction. *Victor W. von Hagen*

Printed in USA

3. The Inca system of terracing in the Colca Valley, southern Peru. These terraces were so well made that they are still in constant use. *Shippee-Johnson aerial photograph, courtesy Wenner-Gren Foundation.*

4. A propitiatory cairn, called *apacheta*, found in all of the high places of Peru on the ancient road. As heavily laden travelers passed along the road, they placed a stone on the *apacheta* as a symbol of the burden, "and so left their tiredness behind." The Persians, the Chinese, and the Greeks adopted more or less the same custom. *Charles Daugherty, Inca Highway Expedition photograph*

5. The ruins of Machu Picchu on the heights overlooking the Urubamba River. A daring example of city planning—a complex of terraces, gabled houses, temples, sacred palaces, and residential compounds. East of Machu Picchu is the jungle. *Victor W. von Hagen, Inca Highway Expedition photograph*

6. Architectural terracing is a feature of Machu Picchu that enabled the inhabitants of this fortified compound to be self-sufficient. The city was unmentioned in Inca annals until discovered in 1911 by the late Hiram Bingham. *Charles Daugherty, Inca Highway Expedition photograph*

7. Road engineering within the Cuzco area. The Inca system of bridging culverts, a form of the corbeled arch, is shown. The road was later placed on top. *Victor W. von Hagen, Inca Highway Expedition photograph*

8. A stone Inca bridge in the Carabaya area (east of Lake Titicaca). It shows an advanced use of the corbeled arch, over an actual distance of thirty feet. The whole is of stone, built about 1450. *Charles Daugherty, Inca Highway Expedition photograph*

9. The northern section of the long Inca coastal road running through Chiquitoy, Chicama Valley, near Trujillo. The Inca road, twenty-four feet wide, bordered by adobe walls (to keep out sand drift), runs past a pre-Inca Mochica pyramid. The coastal road from Tumbes (Peru) to Santiago (Chile) was 2,520 miles long. *Shippee-Johnson aerial photograph, courtesy Wenner-Gren Foundation.*

10. "Tres Cruces" overlooking the Bay of Paracas near Pisco. Dug deep into the sandhill cliffs, 602 feet high, this "Tree of Life" motif occurs often in pre-Inca coastal textiles. Its precise function here is unknown. *Victor W. von Hagen*

11. Square and round built burial *chulpas* (pre-Inca) at Qutimbo, near Lake Titicaca. Chieftains were buried within; there were once so many that a Spaniard in 1547 wrote ". . . they outnumbered the houses of the living. . . ." *Silvia von Hagen, Inca Highway Expedition photograph*

12. Bath of the Chosen Women (*Ñustas*) at Ollantaytambo; an example of rock sculpture, cut from the living rock (*in situ*) and transformed into a fountain. This is a feature of Inca architectural planning. *Victor W. von Hagen, Inca Highway Expedition photograph*

13. An example of pre-Inca tapestry. Three grades of wool cloth were woven and the dyes used yielded such brilliant colors that many articles have been recovered in perfect condition. *Silvia von Hagen*

14. A sculptural ceramic head of a blind man, of the Mochica tribe. Mochica culture, 272 B.C.—A.D. 1000.

15. Man loading a llama. A ceramic from the Mochica culture which maintained llamas on the desert a thousand years before the advent of the Incas. *Victor W. von Hagen*

Part Three

THE INCA AND HIS CITY

22 The Inca

LOUIS XIV, the Sun King of France, actually had to insist that *he* was the state: *"L'état c'est moi."* The Sun King of Peru, the Sapa Inca, never had to emphasize this—all which lay under the sun was his; it was known to everyone and accepted. He was divine, descended by direct line from the Sun, the creator-god; everything—the land, the earth, the people, gold (the sweat of the sun), silver (the tears of the moon)—belonged to him. He was absolute. He was God. His empire was no theoretical theocracy, it was an actual one.

The Lord-Incas were plenary rulers with their powers held in check only by the influence of ancient customs and the fear of revolt. Beyond his exalted position, there was no final court of appeal; the Inca had merely to lift a hand and with that gesture order death to a renowned general or even to a blood relative who had displeased him. The Inca's divinity was very real.

"I remember," said Pedro Pizarro, a cousin of *the* conquistador, "I remember the Lord of Huaylas once asked the Inca [for permission] to visit his estates and it was granted, the Inca giving him limited time in which to go and return. He took rather longer, and when he came back (I was present), brought a gift of fruit and arrived in the Inca's presence. The Lord of Huaylas began to tremble in such a manner before the Inca, that he was unable to remain on his feet. . . ."

If this emotional reaction occurred to one of the most powerful *curacas* of the land, what then must have been the effect of the Inca on mere men, on an Indian who was only a unit in the decimal classification of empire? Yet the con-

113

cern of the Inca for his people, too, was very real; it was not, naturally, as benevolent as that Inca-descended historian, Garcilaso de la Vega, made it out to be when, with the pathos of distance, he wrote his *Royal Commentaries*, nor was it as tyrannical as the Spanish viceroys made it out to be in order to rationalize their destruction of the Inca Empire. The Inca's position and his wealth and his power came from the people and their well-being, for a country does not gain its wealth solely from the numerical quantity of its minerals but from the character and strength of its people. The people and their organization and development within the framework laid down for them were the primary concern of the Inca. All of his officials were held to account for maladministration. A French historian has written of *The Socialist Empire of the Incas*,[7] but this depends on the interpretation of socialism. The land was owned by the state, i.e., the Inca; the Indian, through his *ayllu*, which was a holding corporation, only had use of the land. Yet he owned his chattels, and while he could, theoretically, pile up personal luxury possessions, actually he did not.

An Indian's orbit was restricted; he traveled on the royal roads at the Inca's pleasure; he paid his taxes by labor; even his leisure was ritualistically regimented. Some scholars believe that the Inca, the religion, the state, actually created work artificially as a device of good government to keep the people constantly employed. The Inca, then, demanded *all* from his subjects; in turn he protected them from want, maintained storehouses for prevention of famine, conserved animals and soil. Produce was fairly divided, roads were maintained with superb communications, and the Inca kept the peace within the realm. But it would be a misconception to term this welfare state either socialistic or communistic: the empire was not for the people, and equality was not the ideal; on the contrary, the state existed alone for the Inca.

The Inca's head wife was a *coya* (queen). In the early beginnings of the Inca dynasty the ruler often married into families of other tribes for political alliances. Later, when the Inca was supreme over the land, he married his own sister as his principal wife. The right to marry within the clan belonged only to the Inca. Marriage within the totem group was strictly prohibited. There was an inviolable custom—no one could marry within the first degree. The formal Inca statement was: "We, the Inca, order and decree that no one shall marry his sister or his mother, nor his first cousin, nor his aunt, nor his niece, nor his kinswoman, nor the godmother of his child, under penalty of being punished and of

27. *The litter was the principal transport for the nobility. The Inca and his* coya *(queen) being carried by Rucana tribesmen.*

having his eyes pulled out . . . because only the Inca is allowed to be married to his carnal sister. . . ." [50]

The meaning was obvious: the Incas wanted to insure that their divine descent remained unquestioned, and so from this purity of descent, from the male line of this marriage, came the successor to the "crown."

In addition to his *coya*, the Inca, being polygamous, had many subsidiary wives; the ménage of royal concubines (*pallas*) numbered into the hundreds, and so out of this fecundity flowed immense numbers of descendants of royal, "divine" blood. It is estimated that the last Inca before the conquest had in the male line alone five hundred living descendants; from these were formed the Lord-Inca's immediate family, his own royal *ayllu:* "a useful court circle of educated men trained in the imperial ideology and interested in its perpetuation. The [Lord-Incas] chose their top administrators from this group when possible." [53]

The Incas (like the Romans, in the last days of their empire), had no clear line of succession. The Roman Caesars invariably looked for a suitable successor, trained him for the throne and then adopted him; he became Caesar. The Lord-Incas were also without fixed rule; they named as their successor the most competent of those sons from the principal wife, the *coya.* In one sense this was politic, for the oldest son, as history has repeatedly shown, was not always the most competent, but when the supreme crisis occurred in the empire—the arrival of the Spaniards—a lack of a clear line of descent for an heir apparent laid the base, among other things, for eventual disaster.

Pomp and circumstance surrounded the sons of the Lord-Incas from birth. The smallest things, even such as a haircut, or putting on the breechclout at maturity, were clothed in ritual. Their education was first the study of *Quechua,* the official empire language, then the religion of the Sun (for the Inca was the Sun's vicar on earth, and they had to participate in all of the ritual attendant on it). They had to know the *quipus* so that they as Incas, and intended as administrators, could "read" what the string records said. And finally they learned from the wisemen—*amautas*—Inca history. Since they were expected to lead their people into battle and take active part, as they did, in the new conquests, they spent much time learning the use of arms—the sling, the *macana,* the spear thrower, the bola; they learned the arts of siege, envelop, and mass attack. The sons of the Incas and the nobility undoubtedly followed their elders as they made their rounds of the far-flung empire; this, coupled with the formal education, gave them the experience for governing. At fourteen years, the sons of the nobility assumed the breechclout; a llama was sacrificed, the blood of it smeared on the boy's face. An oath was sworn to the Inca, and the boy received his plaited wool sling, shield, and a silver-headed mace. At the end of the sixth day's ceremony, his ears were pierced, and he became officially a warrior in the Inca's elite guards.

The Inca history which was given out and absorbed by the nobility was the "official line"; it was selective and was no doubt the same as was told to young Garcilaso de la Vega, born in 1539 in Cuzco of a Spanish father and a noble Inca woman: ". . . as a boy . . . I took much delight to hear them tell [the old history] and my relations, being one day upon this conversation of the Inca-Kings and their ancient history, to the oldest of them . . . I asked: 'Inca, my uncle, since there is no writing with you . . . what intelligence have you of the origins and beginnings of our Inca-Kings? . . . You who have no books, what memory have you of our ancient history? Who was the first of the Incas?'" And so this royal person gave the youth, who later wrote the *Royal Commentaries*, the official list of the Inca rulers; since the nobility had a good reason for preserving this memory, those he gave young Garcilaso (and which have been affirmed from many other sources) can be taken as:

1. Manco Capac	7. Yahuar Huacac
2. Sinchi Roca	8. Viracocha Inca
3. Lloque Yupanqui	9. Pachacuti Inca Yupanqui
4. Mayta Capac	10. Topa Inca Yupanqui
5. Capac Yupanqui	11. Huayna Capac
6. Inca Roca	12. Huáscar

13. Atahualpa

Here is the chronology of the later Incas worked out by one of the leading scholars: [53]

1438—Pachacuti crowned
1463—Topa Inca takes command of army
1471—Topa Inca succeeds Pachacuti
1493—Huayna Capac succeeds Topa Inca
1527—Death of Huayna Capac; Huáscar succeeds him
1532—Coming of the Spaniards
1533—Huáscar killed by Atahualpa after long civil war

The Lord-Incas were of Andean origin, sprang from the people, and passed the succession in a continuous line without the introduction of any new aristocracy from the outside. This would not ordinarily have to be stressed, but in the last few years considerable literature has appeared (returning to an old, threadbare theme) suggesting that many of the indigenous American cultures owe their cultural origins to Old World migrations within historical times. The voyage of the balsa raft *Kon-Tiki* from Peru's shores into Polynesia has only exaggerated that which has been current in many scientific circles for many years, i.e., that *all* can be explained by migration. That there *were* sporadic, accidental contacts between Melanesia and America (after the Paleo-Asiatic Mongoloid immigrants crossed to the continent more than twenty-five thousand years ago) can be accepted, but since these contacts brought no exchange of agricultural products, nor exchange of disease, and did not influence either language or physical types, then . . . ! All this "migratory fever" has been ebullient since 1492; the earlier chroniclers believed first that it was Shem, son of Noah, who arrived to populate the land after the deluge; others gave Plato's mythical isle of Atlantis as the source. The celebrated nineteenth-century historian John Ranking, without quitting England's shores, was positive that Manco Capac was a son of Kublai Khan, the first Chinese emperor of the Yuan dynasty, and that he had conquered Peru with a brigade of elephants; this was strengthened by the fact that someone had found bones of the prehistoric mammoth elephants in South America. Incas, it seemed, were of all races: Armenians, Romans, Jews, English, and even Chinese; Arthur Posnansky's monumental work on *Tiahuanacu* is weakened by his insistence that the Chinese language could be understood in certain parts of Bolivia, and that the Inca dynasty was based on the Chinese, which, because of its advanced culture, imposed itself on the politically undeveloped Indians of Peru.

Yet the Lord-Incas in their official history also denied that they came from the people; natural enough, when Western civilization only in the last century quitted the metaphysics of kings by divine right. The history that young Garcilaso de la Vega heard from his uncle, an Inca, is no doubt the official history which all the young nobility learned:

"Cousin," said the old man, "I gladly will tell you, and it behooves you to hear . . . ," and he heard how the Sun God, ". . . seeing men as I have described them, commiserated with them and took pity upon them and sent to earth a son and a daughter to instruct them . . . to give them law . . . and show them how to live in houses and cities. . . ." These two were, of course, the first Inca, Manco Capac, and his sister Mama Ocllo (pronounced "ok-yo"). The Sun God went on in his briefing instructions: ". . . When you have reduced these races [the other Indians, of course, living in the Andes] to your service, you shall maintain them in reason and justice, with benevolence, clemency and kindness. . . . And I therefore appoint and name you Kings, lords of all races. . . ."

There is not the slightest doubt that the Lord-Incas were Andean, were of the same people as they ruled, and were not imposed from without. They invented their own legend of their descent and their divinity, confirming what Anatole France himself wrote of it: ". . . History is not a science, it is an art, and man succeeds in it only by imagination."

The Incas and their "historians" suppressed all historical traditions anterior to the own, and soon the "rememberers," who with their *quipu* knot-string records counted and recounted the history, no longer spoke of anything before the divine Incas; so by a "selective manipulation of history," the Inca nobles grew up with only the knowledge derived from the official point of view. This made them, among other things, thoroughly convinced of their divinity; it was also accepted by the people.

By the time an Inca's descendant was ready to marry, he had as thorough an "education" as one could have in pre-Spanish America. He had accompanied the Inca on tours of the great empire; he had been with the governors who made their rounds; he had taken part in battles either to defend what the Incas had won by arms, or to suppress those who rebelled. He was soaked in ritual and immersed in Inca his-

28. *The Inca's* coya *(queen). She was of royal blood, often his sister, and from among her issue the Inca and his council selected an heir. Redrawn from Felipe Guamán Poma de Ayala.*

tory; he had tasted love in various forms, and had no doubt served some sort of apprenticeship in government so as to gain experience in administration.

His dress, as well as that of the other nobles, was not different in style from the ordinary Indian's—only more sumptuous. His ears were pierced and extended with golden ornaments and jewels; his hair was cut in bangs. His tunic was of the finest alpaca, and often vicuña; his sandals were high and well made.

If the young noble in question was the eldest son of the reigning Inca, born of his first wife, the *coya,* and if it was finally decided by the Inca and his council ("twenty of his relatives," wrote a chronicler, "old and prudent men, full of experience in the government of the kingdom") that this son would be the Inca apparent, sometime toward the end of the Inca's life the son was so designated. The whole empire went into mourning at the Inca's death. His concubines and his personal servants, as in Egypt, were expected, following good custom, to accompany him on his journey to the Sun; they were made drunk, danced, and then were strangled. The Inca's body was partially mummified; the entrails were removed and the vacuity stuffed with cloths. The technique used for mummification in Peru is little or imperfectly known; we have no Herodotus to describe for us the Peruvian system, as he personally observed, for example, the Egyptian. One thing notable is that the Greek word for mummification is *taricheuo,* which means pickling, salting, preserving—and embalming was consciously associated with the curing of fish. The fact that the Inca embalmers removed the viscera of the dead Lord-Inca, the first step toward successful mummification, does suggest the same techniques used for fish preservation.

Mummification was a magico-religious act, and its object in Egypt or in Peru was to keep the body as it was during life for the eventual return of the soul.[19] In the humid uplands of Peru mummification was a technical problem; on the desert Peruvian coast it was different, for the heat of the sun and the naturally sterile, porous sand made the conditions for desiccation and mummification of the dead bodies possible. The Egyptians removed, according to Herodotus, the brain, and viscera, and thoroughly cleaned the cavity with spices, wine, cassia, myrrh; rubbed the outward cadaver with oil, and wrapped it in swathes of cloth. As the Egyptians did, so the embalmers of the divine Inca; they also removed the viscera, which they put into canopic jars, and washed the body.

Nothing much else is known of the embalming, nor precisely how the royal mummies appeared, for they were the first things looted by the conquistadors. The mummy (*malquis*) of the dead Inca was placed in his house, and a life-size golden statue (*pucarina*) was made of him; it was served with food as though he still lived. He sat on his golden stool, which was the symbol for a throne. There are few descriptions of these mummies; some were carried away by Manco Capac II when the young Inca rose in revolt against the Spaniards in 1536 and fled into the vastness of Vilcapampa. In 1559 a Spanish official found the mummified bodies of three of the Incas. The Spanish viceroy ordered their removal from Cuzco to Lima, where they subsequently disappeared.*

The new Inca, after fasting for three days, was crowned. It was not really a "crown" but a fringe. There were, as on all occasions such as this, pomp, dancing, drinking; obeisance was made to the dead Inca, and the new Lord-Inca started, as was the custom, to build himself a new elaborate house in the center of Cuzco. (That of his predecessor, the deceased Inca, had become *huaca*, or shrine.) His principal wife, long acquired, now was his *coya*. Secondary wives were acquired, urged on him by other members of the select circle of nobility; concubines came to him from among the Chosen Women. He set the policy of his reign, and acquired many of the honorific titles of his father—Sapa Inca, "Shepherd of the Sun" (*Intip Curi*), "Lover of the Poor"— and he began to act like the divinity that he was.

The Inca "received" seated on a golden stool (*osño*); his visitors were barefooted and weighed down with a symbolic burden to suggest submission. All of his governing *curacas* prostrated themselves when they came before him.

As Inca, he was surrounded by a retinue of elaborate ritual. He ate from gold and silver services, placed upon finely woven mats; his Chosen Women held the plates as he ate. The uneaten food was put aside and stored to be burned later with ceremony, along with his clothes, which he never donned twice. He slept on a raised paillasse covered with colorfully woven woolens, and attended by numbers of his women. As befitted a god, he rarely walked for long distances: when he led a battle he was carried on the royal litter; when he made a tour of the empire, which could well

---

* As related by Garcilaso de la Vega (Lib. v cxxix). The three bodies of Lord-Incas were Viracocha (*d.* 1400?); Topa Inca Yupanqui (*d.* 1493); and Huayna Capac (*d.* 1527). They were found with two of their wives in a perfect state of preservation. They were borne through the streets of Lima and interred in the courtyard of the hospital of San Andrés in the year 1562.

occupy years, he was borne in his royal palnaquin. "They traveled in great majesty," wrote Pedro de Cieza de León, ". . . seated in rich litters, fitted with loose poles of excellent wood, and enriched [i.e., covered by plate] with gold and silver. Over the litter there were two high arches of gold set with precious stones. . . ." Because of the precipitous terrain, despite the excellence of the roads, he traveled ponderously, no more than twelve miles the day. A large retinue of officials went with him and the people were gathered along the road to see him. There was always in attendance on him a company of litter-bearers, the Rucanas—a sturdy people who lived west of Cuzco—attired in a special blue livery; they changed in relays of eight. There is little doubt about

29. *An Inca general riding in a litter using the sling. This hurled an egg-sized stone fifty yards with accuracy.*

the magnificence of these litters, for when Francisco Pizarro, *the* conquistador, entered Cuzco, he found one in the tombs of the mummified Incas; by his contract with the King of Spain he was allowed to select one of these for himself, which he considered the most precious object of his loot.

The Lord-Inca was accoutered as his people: tuniclike poncho, breechclout, sandals, all magnificently woven in vicuña wool by his Chosen Women. His ear spools were immense, gold and jeweled; his hair was cut in bangs and he carried a golden-headed mace. There seems to have been an imperial standard, a pennant stiffened with dyestuff on which a symbol was painted. His crown was a royal fringe called *llautu* (pronounced "lyaw-to"), made of red wool and worn wrapped around the head. A fringe of red tassels lined with gold lamé hung down before the eyes. An eyewitness to the conquest saw the Inca wearing ". . . on his head a '*llautos*,' which are braids made of colored wools, half a finger thick and a finger in breadth, made in the form of a crown, rounded and without points, a hand's width, which fitted his head, the forehead a tassel called a borla . . . adorned very subtly with bangles of gold".[49]

The last Inca before the conquest, Atahualpa (apart from those puppet Incas placed on the royal throne-stool by their conquerors), is the only Lord-Inca whose personal description we have: "He was well set up for an Indian, of good presence, medium figure, not over stout, comely of countenance and serious withall, his eyes florid . . . much feared by his people . . ."[49] And fastidious: "One day as he was eating . . . while raising a piece of food to his mouth it dropped onto the robe he was wearing . . . he quickly rose and retired to the inner chamber and returned wearing an under-robe and a dark brown mantle,"[49] made of bat skins. And of unchallenged power: "Nor have I seen in all this Peru an Indian like unto this Atahualpa either for his fierceness or for his air of authority."[49]

There is no doubt about the sumptuousness of the Inca's world; archaeology has confirmed it. The gold that did not disappear into the crucible of the conquistadors confirms all that had been first said about it. Tombs have yielded gold-spangled litters, superb examples of feather weaving and woven tapestries which hang today in the world's most famous museums. The pottery from Peru is superior in form and variety to anything that the ancient world can offer. Those historians of the "natural school" who accused William Prescott, who worked from the original sources, of "romanticism," of painting too glamorous a picture of Inca

30. *A curaca or governor, learning from a* quipu *reader the amount of food stored in the stone storage bins.*

ceremonial life, have been gainsaid; all has been affirmed by archaeology.

In his realm the Inca was absolute. As the Sapa Inca he ruled this immense land, which was called Tawantinsuyu, "Land of the Four Directions"; he used the nobility who were Incas by blood, or those Indians who had raised themselves by their qualities to become Incas by privilege (as England does by raising commoners of merit to the nobility).

The Incas, just as the common Indians, had their own royal *ayllus;* from them came the Incas by blood. They formed the ruling classes, and from them the Inca chose his administrators. They had their ears pierced. Pierced ears marked the nobility. The small hole in the ear lobe was gradually enlarged until an egg could pass through it; into this the Incas placed a rounded golden and jeweled disk. The

Spaniards called this class "Big Ears," and as *Orejones* they have entered the literature. They went about their labors bejeweled and bedecked. They were polygamous, with many wives and concubines. They had other special privileges; they paid no taxes, yet they were a functional aristocracy. All their duties, which demanded much travel in this perpendicular world, were taken very seriously; there is no evidence in the chronicles of any sybaritic idleness. If they did not carry out the Inca's orders, they answered for it with their heads.

The second class of administrators were Incas by privilege, those called *curacas,* who were not necessarily born in the royal *ayllus* but whose ability pulled them upward. Because the Incas extended their empire so rapidly, they did not have the number of Incas by blood needed for administrative purposes; often a conquered land had its own chieftain confirmed in his rule, while his sons were whisked off to Cuzco for an orientation course and returned as *curacas.* All were exempt from taxation, i.e., the work tax: they drew their emoluments from the service (*mita*) of the common Indian. These Incas by privilege accoutered themselves in sumptuous feather tunics, the kind that are now unearthed from tombs; they had their ears pierced and decorated with golden spools; they selected their wives from the Chosen Women; they were bound by loyalty to the Inca because of his bestowal of office. And the capital, the heart of this empire which sent its life-streams pulsating in the four cardinal directions, the famous mecca of the entire realm was—Cuzco.

23 *Cuzco*

THE FEELINGS of men have founded cities. Men have fallen on their knees when they came to a place where something within them came to rest; they have built a capital in a desert where it is not possible for a city to be; an emperor has *loved* a place of the earth and made it a great city." [31]

Cuzco was such a place. The founding of it by the legendary first Inca, Manco Capac, is placed circa A.D. 1100. Cuzco was, it will be recalled from Inca myths, the place where Manco Capac rested after his wanderings from the south and where the golden staff given to him by the Sun God disappeared when he threw it into the ground. Precisely whom the Incas displaced is not known; the pre-Inca cultures within Cuzco are referred to as merely "Chanapata." Yet there is no reason to doubt the history of the city as it is given by the Incas; archaeology is in agreement that its culture developed within its immediate valley.

Cuzco lies in the hollow of a valley at about 11,000 feet. On three of its sides the mountains rise precipitously, and at its southeast the valley yawns widely and stretches for miles between a double array of mountains, a succession of fertile plains and bog. Two small rivers flow down into it, and in Inca times these were canalized with finely worked stone; buildings were erected on the banks.

Cuzco was divided into two parts: Hanan, or Upper Cuzco, and Hurin, or Lower Cuzco. In the latter part, the capital center, the nobles had their houses. There were two main plazas from which narrow streets issued. "It was grand and stately," wrote one who saw it in its glory, "and must have been founded by a people of great intelligence. It has fine streets, except that they are narrow, and the houses are built of solid stones, beautifully joined. . . . [Cuzco] was richest of which we have any knowledge in all the Indies, for the great store of treasures was often brought to increase the grandeur of the nobles. . . ." [14]

Only five Europeans, one of whom was Hernando de Soto, saw Cuzco before it was raped of its gold and before it was partially destroyed by the wars, and they have left no report. Cuzco's archaeology is imperfectly known.

126

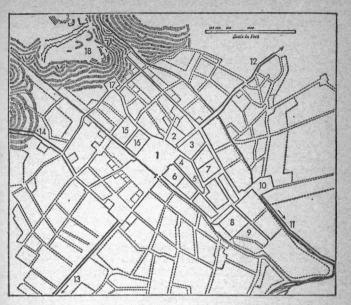

31. *Cuzco, the capital of the Inca realm as it probably appeared in* A.D. 1500.
1) In the center of the city, Huaycapata (Joy Square). 2) Palace of Viracocha Inca. 3) Hatuncancha. 4) Palace of Huáscar. 5) Acclahuasi, Temple of the Virgins. 6) Amarucancha, Palace of Huayna Capac. 7) Palace of Topa Inca Yupanqui. 8) Temple of the Sun. 9) Curicancha ("Golden Enclosure"). 10) Rimacpampa. 11) Road to the south, the Collasuyu quarter. 12) Road to the east, the jungle or Antisuyu quarter. 13) Road to the west, the Cuntisuyu quarter. 14) Road to the north toward Quito, the Chinchasuyu quarter. 15) Yuchayhuasi, schools of the nobles. 16) Cora-Cora, Palace of Inca Roca. 17) Palace of Manco Capac. 18) Fortress of Sacsahuamán.

Cuzco, as a city, emerged in final form when it was rebuilt after A.D. 1400, and it showed good town planning. At this time the two rivers that entered from the north were canalized. There was a gridiron scheme for streets, converging out of two central plazas. The houses of the meaner sort were one-storied, but others, the greater ones, were two-storied, and sometimes three stories in height. The principal buildings were located about the great plaza, and the towering Sun Temple occupied the most prominent part. To retain its purity, water was conveyed with great care through stone conduits laid in the middle of the street.

Out from the principal plaza, called Huaycapata ("Joy Square"), spread the twelve wards of the city, divided roughly into four sections—the four principal directions or quarters of the world which gave the empire its name, Tawantinsuyu.

Cuzco actually was a microcosm of empire; within it lived people drawn from many parts, all attired in traditional dress. "Each tribe," explained Cieza de León, who saw them, "is distinguished by differences in headdress; if they are *Yungas* from the coast, they went muffled like gypsies; the *Collas* [from around Lake Titicaca] wore caps in the shape of a plump box of wool; while the *Canas* [now the village of Tinta] wore another cap, larger and of greater width. The *Cañaris* [from the province of Cañar in faraway Ecuador] had crowns of thick lathes, like those used for a sieve. The *Huancas* [i.e., "Field Guardians" who were centered about Jauja, in mid-Peru] had short ropes which hung down as low as the chin, with the hair plaited. The *Canchis* [modern Sicuani was their center] had wide fillets of red or black passing over the forehead. All of these tribes were distinguished particularly by their form of headdress, so clear and distinct that when fifteen thousand men assembled, one tribe could be easily distinguished from another." In point of fact, the Inca ruled that all tribesmen should keep their distinctive headdress.

These were some of the inhabitants of Cuzco, all quartered in their local sections, occupying low houses of sun-baked mud, painted red or yellow and thatched with thick straw. The King of Spain's inspector said that there were 100,000 houses in the city—obviously an exaggeration—he perhaps meant the number of people—yet he affirmed that "in the eight days [that he was there], I have not been able to see everything." [17]

The Sun Temple, the edifices of the Lord-Incas, the Chosen Women, and others were constructed by professional architects and were the pride of the realm. They were defined by long reaches of stones elaborately cut and fitted with a precision which has never been duplicated anywhere in the world. The exteriors of the buildings (unlike the Maya or Aztec buildings, which were floriated with design) were seldom if ever decorated; the more important ones were sheathed with gold plate. The first Spaniard to see Cuzco—it seemed abalze with gold—reported he saw a "quadrangular building . . . measuring three hundred and fifty paces from corner to corner, entirely plated with gold; of these gold plates they took down seven hundred which together weighed five hundred pesos of gold. . . ." [17] Much of the golden loot from Cuzco was plate torn from the walls: "These had been taken from the walls . . . they had holes in them showing that they had been secured by nails," showing that many of the royal edifices in Cuzco had been gold-plated.[14] At least enough to make the high sententious fantasy of the conquistador soar.

Cuzco, with all these gold-spangled walls, could not have been less spectacular than those cities which Marco Polo looked upon in Cathay, whose walls were covered with gold a good finger in thickness, and whose towers of silver and gold were girt about with bells.

Not only was Cuzco filled with tribesmen from all parts of the realm, each with their distinctive headgear, but here too resided the chieftains of other tribes which the Incas had absorbed, giving the city an Arabian Nights' unreality. The chieftains of the Chimús were here, with pierced nose septum from which jangled gold and emeralds, their heads wound high with plaited turbans. They were the Incas by privilege in enforced residence. Although treated royally, they were actually hostages to insure that their recently conquered territory allowed itself to be absorbed, and their sons were enrolled in the schools of the nobles to be reoriented in the new order of the Inca.

There were royal storehouses throughout the city, filled with tribute from all of the subject states: cotton was piled high from the coast; there were others with seashells and seaweed; some held arms for war. Cuzco was also an arsenal of quilted cotton armor, sharp-edged swords, star-shaped battle axes, slings, and javelins.

The royal artisans were located here too, the "professionals," nontaxpayers who worked for the Lord-Inca's pleasure by turning out fabulously cast gold and silver pieces, and, as averred by Pedro de Cieza de León: "There were a great many of gilders and workers in silver who understood how to work the things ordered by the Incas . . . and no gold nor silver might be taken out on the pain of death. . . ."

Cuzco was certainly a most magnificently planned city, of which there have been few counterparts in the world. The most fabulous edifice in Cuzco was the Curi-cancha, "Golden Enclosure," at the spot where legend said stood the first edifice erected by the first Inca. The conquistadors who saw it never tired of telling of what they saw, and after five hundred years archaeologists are still trying to piece together this most stupefying, ancient, and sacred of Inca shrines. The Temple of the Sun adjoined the Golden Enclosure. It was a shrine as well as a center for the priestly organization. It was presided over by the "chief priest *Huillac-Umu* who lived in the grand temple." This complex structure had six major buildings: sanctuaries to the Sun, Moon, Stars, Lightning,

Rainbow, and a sort of chapter house for the priests of the Sun; all these various parts surrounded the Inti Pampa, "Field of the Sun." A fountain in its vast center was encased in gold on which was etched the image of the Sun, the same Sun which fell to the conquistador who gambled it away one night. The outside of the building (parts of which can now still be seen as part of the Church of Santo Domingo set on top of the Inca one) was covered with gold plate so massive that each sheet weighed from four to ten pounds. Although the roof was thickly thatched with grass, it also had, reportedly, golden straws among the others, which caught the rays of the sun's declension with each day.

To the utter amazement of the first Europeans to see it, the Curi-cancha had in its fields a golden mimicry of plants: maize, actual size, was "planted" and its stalks cunningly wrought in gold, and Cieza tells of the "garden where the clods [of earth] were pieces of fine gold, and it was artificially sown with cornfields which were of gold, as well as the stems of the leaves and the [corn] cobs. Besides all this they had more than twenty llamas of gold with their young, and the [Indian] shepherds life-size, with their slings and crooks to watch them . . . all made of gold." There is no doubting this report, for the King of Spain's inspector, Miguel de Estete, attached to the expedition to attest officially to the items of loot received, recorded that he saw "straws made of solid gold, with their spikes just as they grow in the fields. And if I was to recount all the different varieties in the shape of gold my story would never end. . . ."

Certainly the simulated vines with grapes or bunches of precious stones which were given to Darius the Persian by Pythias, and described so wonderfully by that wandering Greek, Herodotus, could not be compared to this whole Field of the Sun at Cuzco, planted with a golden garden; nor can the famous "Ram Caught in a Thicket" which was found in the royal tombs at Ur (dating from 2500 B.C.), a piece of polychrome statuary covered with thin gold foil nineteen inches high, even be compared to twenty life-size figures of llamas of cast gold, which grazed on golden stalks of grass in the Golden Enclosure of Cuzco.

It strains the imagination, at this distance in time, to accept all this as coming out of the indigenous American cultures, without contact with the old; but a visit to any of the museums which contain ancient Peruvian collections (bearing in mind that the best was melted down in the crucibles of the conquest) will convince even the most skeptical of the organization that this barbaric empire must have had.

But it must be repeated that the form of organization

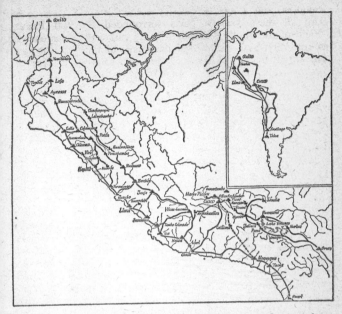

32. *Capacñan, the royal road of the Incas. The network of roads as recorded by the von Hagen Expedition (1952-54). The series of roads issuing from Cuzco ran more or less in the four cardinal directions to the four quarters of the realm. Prepared from the explorations of the author. Redrawn by Pablo Carrera.*

within the four quarters of the empire was only an *intensified* development of the original pre-Inca patterns. This specialization of Indian labor made possible the great achievements of the Inca Empire.

Part Four

THE ACHIEVEMENTS

24 Inca Architecture

INCA ARCHITECTURE, as all great architectural styles, developed out of the rustic houses of the peasants. This was as true in Greece as it was in Peru. The most awe-inspiring of Inca structures—the cyclopean walls of polished stonework—are only a development of the one-room house of the common Indian, the kind which proliferated at random throughout the Andes at the beginning of the Inca realm.

These houses, placed in a square with a common yard (*cancha*), developed into the rectangular city plan of the Incas, and no matter how imposing the Inca building, it suggests always its humble origin. "For," writes Dr. John Rowe, developing this viewpoint, "even the most complex of Inca buildings in the finest masonry never became much more than a group of such houses [the native houses of field stone grouped to form a *cancha*], conveniently and usually rather regularly disposed within an enclosure wall. It is an architecture which like the Quechua language consists of irreducible units grouped together in complex but irregular patterns, but never quite losing their identity." [54]

The Incas are famed for the quantity and variety of their stone structures, but few have ever emphasized the sheer quantity of the mass of buildings that existed; it is true that much centers about Cuzco, yet much lies outside it.

At the height of the Inca Empire, say, A.D. 1500, Inca structures spread over an enormous distance—from the Sun temples and fortress of Purumauca on the north bank of the Maule River (35° S. lat.) in southern Chile, north to the Ancasmayo River (approximately 1° N. lat.), which is now in Colombia—3,250 linear miles.

Along this route were large centers (*marcas*), replete with

132

administrative centers and Sun temples; there were stone-laid palaces, temples for Sun Virgins, official storehouses, and fortresses. Along the entire web of roads, *tampu* way stations appeared every four to twelve miles, so that for the sheer mass of building, the empire almost equaled the Roman.

At the height of Egypt's Middle Kingdom, to give historical comparison, its structures covered a distance of only 625 miles, that is from Alexandria at the delta of the Nile to the rapids of Aswan, and then this land was only a narrow width within the same desert environment. So that the mass of Inca building, spreading over a diverse terrain, varying, as has been shown, from desert to high altitudes to jungle, is more than five times the distance of the Egyptian empire. Within this immense geographical span there was a uniformity of style and purpose of building marking it all "Inca." While it is true, and the theme has been constantly hammered home, that much of the Inca civilization was borrowed, nevertheless the Inca brought all the congeries of geography together and gave its culture an architectonic unity.

The city—better, the idea of the city—is not much more than six thousand years old. Earthbound Neolithic man, then living in self-contained villages, formed an idea of the city. V. Gordon Childe has called this the "Urban Revolution." Though the American people were out of the broad stream of Eurasian evolution (a strong current from which all culture in the Old World drew), they none the less instinctively followed this selfsame pattern. The city everywhere, whether it was in the valleys of the Nile, or in Greece, Egypt, in Sumeria, or even among the Incas exhibited the same dynamic features: specialized labor, intensified production, disciplined organization, the construction of temples, palaces, pyramids, tombs, and other symbols of the collective imagination. The Inca city, of which Cuzco was the supreme example, had all these; one architectural writer thinks, "The Incas were the best planners South America ever knew . . . [After] four hundred years of European domination . . . the urban spirit of the Incas still pervades Cuzco and many smaller towns in the region." [67] The form of Cuzco is more or less the city plan which the Inca's professionals imposed upon the realm: the gridiron scheme of streets converging on a central plaza with the principal buildings located about it; the large square; the truncated Sun Temple pyramid, with buildings around it housing the priests of the Sun; a palace for the visiting Inca; houses of the Virgins of the Sun; and an administration center. The houses of the people were arranged in the rectangular *cancha*-style.

There were no walled Inca cities. Each large city had, if it was built close to a hill, which it usually was, a fortress, called *pucara*, and within there was a miniature of the city it guarded. When attacked, the people were expected to go up to it with their weapons and from there defend themselves.

All this architecture came from central planning. In the extent of this type of realm, that is, in three thousand miles, there was, and still remains, a great variety of forms of architecture, and enough survives to gain a fair idea of what this civic-military planning appeared to be. To give some of these significant examples, one can begin at *Ayaviri*, around the northern end of Lake Titicaca at a place then, as now, of considerable importance.

"In ancient times," wrote Pedro de Cieza de León, "[Ayaviri] was a grand thing to see . . . and this place [in 1549] is still worthy of note . . . The Lord-Inca Yupanqui ordered that a great palace should be built there . . . together with many buildings where the tribute was stored up. A Temple of the Sun was also built. . . ."

Fifty miles north of this center, on the royal road (between the intervals of which were many smaller communities) was *Cacha*, "where there were great edifices . . . a temple built in memory of their god [Tici] Viracocha." [14] This city stands on the right bank of the Yucay River about forty-eight miles from Cuzco. The temple, one of the most unusual of Inca structures, was dominated by a row of round columns on its two sides. The structure, which has been in the most part destroyed, still has walls of beautifully worked stone at the base, adobe as it rises; it was straw-thatched and must have been equivalent to one of our buildings three stories in height. ("Within it there was a stone idol, the height of a man, with a robe and crown.") [14] Going out from this remarkable structure there are a series of formal streets with houses capped with gabled roofs. Beside it, and plainly to be seen still, runs the royal road, eighteen feet wide. Here appears the architectural impress of the Incas—the trapezoidal niche—and it appears wherever they set foot; it is the dominant architectural decoration and is in effect the leitmotif of the Incas.

Urban centers of formal nature, plazas bordered with Sun temples and palaces (yet changing to fit the geography) are found all along the royal roadway toward Cuzco. There is a formal gateway at *Rumicolca*, twenty-one miles from the capital of Cuzco. The hills about are studded with ruins, Inca and pre-Inca; the sites keep to the plan. And in those

intervening miles between the formal entrance to the valley
and Cuzco itself there are, or were, many others.

Cuzco itself, as has already been said, was the focal
point of the empire, and within it are to be seen walls dating

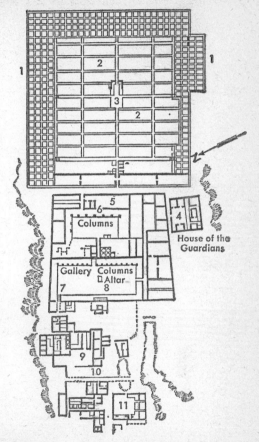

33. Plan No. 1 *of the ruins of Incahuasi (Runahuanac or
Lunahuaná), built circa* A.D. *1450 in the Cañete valley
(Huarco). Redrawn from Emilio Harth-terré.*
1) Granaries, for storing corn, beans, sea food. 2) Drying
platforms for food. 3) Administration center for food
operations. 4) House of the Guardians. 5) House complex,
presumably for chieftain. 6) Columns. 7) Gallery with
ascending steps. 8) Altar. 9) Habitations. 10) Street,
showing evidence of paving. 11) Habitations.

from the different epochs of its architectural history. The Incas emphasized that which Frank Lloyd Wright has termed "integral architecture"—the livable interior space of the room. In integral architecture, "the room space itself must

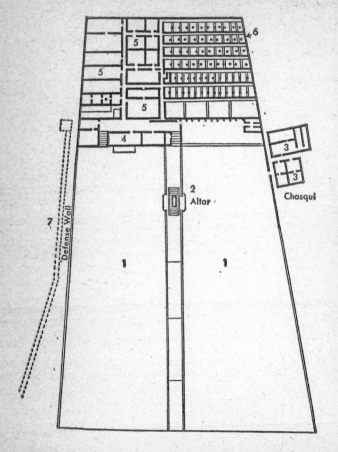

34. Plan No. 2 *of the ruins of Incahuasi. Redrawn from Emilio Harth-terré.*
1) Trapezoid-shaped plaza (typical in Inca town planning), site of religious pageants. 2) Altar (with steps), where high-priest conducted the "mysteries." 3) House of the Chasquis (road couriers). 4) Guards' house. 5) Habitations, possibly for chieftains. 6) Halls of the columns (an unusual feature in Inca architecture). 7) Wall, either for defense or against possible flash flood from dry river.

come through, the room must been as architecture." This is fully apparent in Inca architecture.

They used no nails, no wood, except the poles held together with withes to serve as base for the thickly thatched roof. Although the corbeled arch was known and used in bridges, it was almost never used in the large buildings. The placing of the small niche window and the large stone door (see Plate I) is a miracle of proportion and symmetry.

Next in the architectural parade is *Pisac*, twenty-one miles northeast of Cuzco; it guarded the upper Urubamba River. On the pinnacle of a rock massif stands, or better hangs, Pisac and its agricultural terraces. The Inca's engineers took advantage of this natural fortress, separated from the rest of the massif by deep gorges, to construct an amazing series of defensive forts, tunnels, walls, and gateways. Many of the important structures in the sacred part of the city of Pisac, i.e., the part built about the so-called sundial (*Inti-huatana*, "hitching place of the sun"), were built upon the outcrops of the living rock; the marvelously wrought stones fitted, in a perfect concourse, into this living rock, forming what Wright, that demiurge of modern building, called "organic architecture." It is the "nature of an organic architecture to grow from its site, come out of the ground into the light."

There is nothing quite like Pisac in the entire range of the Inca realm.

Yet, farther down this gorge, is *Ollantaytambo* ("Posthouse of Ollantay"), twenty-four miles northwest of Cuzco and set near to the upper Urubamba River. It was first a village; then in 1460 it was rebuilt as a fortress to protect against the incursions of tribes from the Antisuyu (northeastern quarter of the empire) advancing on Cuzco. There is a famous local legend which identifies Ollantay with the lover of an Inca princess, perhaps the best-known example of "Inca literature" (see page 569). Since the present-day village is set over the old one, it has been a favorite place for the study of Inca architecture, for the site still is one of the finest examples extant of Inca town planning.

The old part of the city is composed of a large plaza laid out like a gridiron, and rising above is an acropolis of rock with an enormous fortress (*pucara*) built on its sides; cut into the living rock itself are agricultural terraces. It was being built when the Spaniards arrived in 1536; work was stopped, and one can still see the immense stones lying where they were abandoned. The present-day village, dating from 1540, was built into and around Ollantay. The streets are narrow, the walls bounded by beautiful lines of masonry, so com-

plete that one can form a fairly clear idea of this type of
Inca town planning. Houses (*wasi*) constructed of stone
foundations and adobe are built into a group and surrounded
by a wall, the *cancha*, essential base of all complex Inca
architecture. The fortress is built on top of the acropolis
and frowns over the city; a massive stone stairway leads to
the top. Here there are six famous megalithic stones which
were to form the base of the Sun Temple, and a wall behind
the fortress (which has a number of dwelling places and storage rooms) completes the fortress acropolis. On the other
side of the Urubamba River are quarries; a road zigzags up
the steep sides, and from here the Indian miners quarried the
rock masses. Still to be seen are the rude houses of the workers, and the valley is full of half-worked stones.

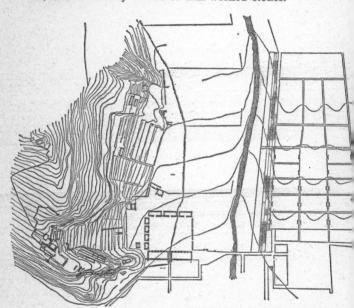

35. *Ollantaytambo, twenty-four miles northwest of Cuzco, on the
upper Urubamba River. This typifies the "ideal" Inca urban planning:
the self-contained city, formed of a series of* cancha *complexes, and
above it, the* pucara *or fortress.*

Farther down this Urubamba gorge, high on the top of the
V-shaped valley, are a series of stone-laid cities which constituted a veritable chain of fortress-sanctuaries, built, it is
believed, to defend the empire from raids of the wilder

tribes of the jungles. They are built about fifteen hundred feet above the gorge of the river and seem to be hanging. These fortress complexes, known in succession as Huaman-marca, Patallacta, Winay-whayna, Botamarca, Loyamarca, terminate in the most spectacular one of all—the well-known *Machu Picchu*.[18] All of these are bound together by a stone-laid road. They are approximately ten miles apart. At Machu Picchu the Urubamba River cascades onward and downward to the humid jungles.

Machu Picchu is so well known it hardly need be repeated that until its discovery in 1911 by the late Hiram Bingham, it was never mentioned by Inca or Spaniard. It was as if it had been left by its last inhabitants, so that here we have—almost without parallel in any other culture (if one excepts the ruins of Pompeii and Herculaneum)—an undisturbed picture of what such a corporate village looked like before it was changed or "restored" by those who added their personal equation to history.

The ruins of Machu Picchu (no one knows what its original name was) lie in a topographical saddle between the peaks of Machu (Old) Picchu and Huayna (New) Picchu. In this "saddle is a complex of terraces, gabled houses, temples, sacred plazas and residential compounds." [70]

Machu Picchu is essentially a fortified city; its strongly constructed houses were most probably defense units. Here there *was* a wall, one of the few walled places in Inca architecture. It had one stone entrance, with a massive wooden gate (an eye-bonder projected from the stone lintel to support it), and it had a small perpendicular stone pin to secure the hole to lock the gate. Machu Picchu was, like most *Pucaras* (city defense units), a self-sustaining unit. There are here, as elsewhere in the Inca Empire, various styles of architecture; the royal palaces made of well-fitted granite ashlars, crude clan houses for the common people, barracks for soldiers. All houses were thatched with grass roofs, very thick and possibly of long duration; [10] the interiors of the houses were Spartan in their severity. Such is Machu Picchu, the terminus, it seems, of a constellation of hanging cities, joined by a stone-laid road (the best of the Roman imperial ways was laid no better) to the center of the empire—Cuzco.

Why were these cities built in the later days of the realm; what purpose this vast expenditure of labor? There was no shortage of land—the Inca conquests spread over a quarter of South America—but these hanging cities did not provide much in the matter of what the Germans would call *Lebensraum* (living space), for if the available space for crops is measured at Machu Picchu, it could not have sup-

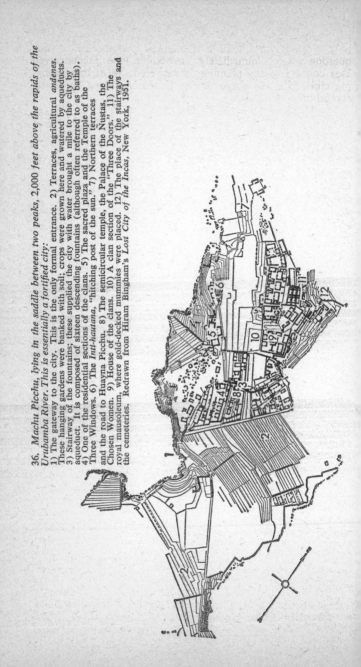

36. *Machu Picchu, lying in the saddle between two peaks, 2,000 feet above the rapids of the Urubamba River. This is essentially a fortified city:*
1) The gateway to the city. This is the only formal entrance. 2) Terraces, agricultural *andenes*. These hanging gardens were banked with soil; crops were grown here and watered by aqueducts. 3) Stairway of the fountains; these supplied the city with water brought a mile to the city by aqueduct. It is composed of sixteen descending fountains (although often referred to as baths). 4) One of the residential sections of the clans. 5) The sacred plaza and the Temple of the Three Windows. 6) The *Inti-huatana*, "hitching post of the sun." 7) Northern terraces and the road to Huayna Picchu. 8) The semicircular temple, the Palace of the Nustas, the Chosen Women. 9) House of the clans. 10) A clan section of the "Three Doors." 11) The royal mausoleum, where gold-decked mummies were placed. 12) The place of the stairways and the cemeteries. Redrawn from Hiram Bingham's *Lost City of the Incas*, New York, 1951.

ported much more than five hundred people! Yet if this question is not immediately answerable, the preconceived Inca concept of city planning is answered: all of these hanging cities over the gorge of the Urubamba show the same careful urban base plan.

Northwest of these, in a different valley and on a direct line to Cuzco, is *Limatambo* (actually in Incan times Rimactampu), lying in the frigid shadow of Mount Salcantay, 20,000 feet high. Limatambo was the way station before "the Great Speaker," the Apurimac River, one of the royal stations on the great 1,250-mile-long arterial road between Cuzco and Quito. Like the finest buildings of Cuzco, it is constructed in the polygonal style, large, irregularly shaped stones faced according to natural contours, and with such accuracy that the finest blade cannot be pushed between them. What remains of Limatambo again shows town planning.

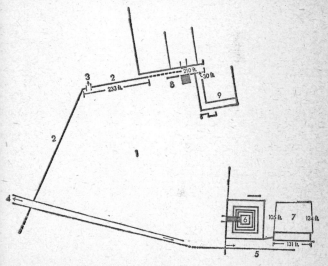

37. *Vilcas-huamán. This city, the most important between Cuzco and Jauja, directly on the royal road of the Incas, was believed by the Incas to be the "center" of their realm, that is the distance from here to Chile was the same as the distance from here to Quito.*
1) The plaza. 2) Wall which enclosed the plaza. 3) Road to Cuntisuyu (northwest). 4) Road to Cuzco. 5) Road to Quito. 6) Sun Temple.
7) Residence of the Sun priests. 8) Curi-cancha ("Golden Enclosure").
9) Residence of Inca Huayna Capac.

Still continuing on the royal road and a hundred miles northward is *Vilcas-huamán*, at 11,000 feet altitude. "The

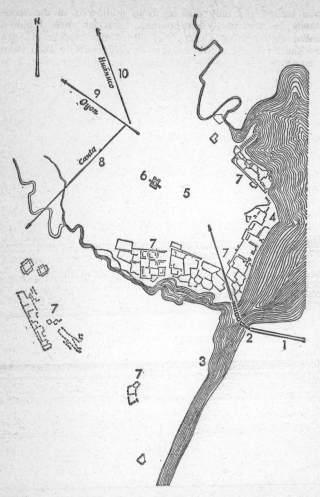

38. *Bonbón or* Pumpu, *a large center near Lake Junín. It is typical of later Inca urban planning.*
1) Road from Cuzco. 2) Suspension bridge. 3) Mantaro River. 4) Lake Junín. 5) Plaza. 6) Sun Temple. 7) Dwellings. 8) Road to Canta and Pacific Coast. 9) Road to Oyon and Callejon de Huaylas. 10) Road to Quito via Huánuco.

Hawk's Sanctuary" lies on the high Vilcas plateau above the Vischongo River. Here a stone-laid, truncated Sun Temple still stands, the only one of those numbered in the thousands to survive. Vilcas-huamán, although two hundred miles distant from Cuzco, has all of the aspects of Inca architecture, and shows the striking uniformity in Inca town planning. There is an immense plaza ("large enough to hold," said Pedro de Cieza de León, who had apparently seen it then, "fifty thousand people"). It is bordered to the west by the Sun Temple, to the east by the palace of the Inca; the House of the Virgins of the Sun occupied another corner, and in another section were the royal storage chambers. The streets were narrow and paved and were lined with houses.

Three roads of empire coming from different directions met in the plaza. The Sun Temple (see Plate I) is now as it was described by Cieza de León: "made of very fine fitting stones with two large doorways (on opposite sides), with two stairways leading up from them with thirty-three steps . . . and on its truncated top one hundred feet above the plaza . . . a large stone seat [once gold-plated], where the Lord-Inca sat to view the dances and festivals. . . ."

Inca architecture was functional. There were no structures in the length of the realm that had the human uselessness of the pyramids, of the kind which gave Julian Huxley "no aesthetic pleasure," * and which he thought to be the quintessential of conspicuous waste.[30]

Once again northward, three hundred miles from the last mentioned Inca center, is little-known *Bonbón* at a land height of 12,500 feet. Here, as in Vilcas-huamán, three arterial roads met in a large plaza. A suspension bridge spanned the river, the Mantaro, an approach road came through rows of houses—of the common sort (field stone cemented together with adobe mud and thatched with grass)—and the street debouched into an enormous trapezoid-shaped plaza. In the center stood the Sun Temple; along three of its sides were an impressive number of houses which were gabled and grass-thatched. The roads of empire converged here, passed by the Sun Temple, and went on into the void of the Andes.

On the same road, which goes between Cuzco and Quito, and another hundred miles northward, is *Huánuco*. It is, or was, immense. Still to be seen is the outline of its square plaza, reached on all its four sides by a flight of stone steps. "Huánuco has a fine royal palace," said Pedro de Cieza, ". . . near it a Temple of the Sun with many virgins and priests. It was so grand a place in the time of the Incas that

* Actually he was speaking here of Persia and its jewel-encrusted swords.

more than thirty thousand Indians were set apart solely for its service." The buildings that housed all these people, as well as the temples, are still to be seen. Again three roads of empire came into the plaza and left in different directions.

And still the architectural parade marches on. One would be bored with a repetition of it; how at *Cajamarca*, two hundred miles farther north (and where the last Lord-Inca Atahualpa was captured, held for ransom, and executed), there was yet another Inca center, planned as all the rest. Lying at 8,500 feet in altitude, half-way between Cuzco and Quito, it was small as Inca centers go; still the Spaniards who first saw it on Friday, November 15, 1532, found its plaza "larger than any in Spain," surrounded by a high wall and entered by two doorways which opened upon the streets of the town. The buildings were long, strongly built, "three times the height of a man and roofed with straw."

"They were," the king's inspector went on, "the finest we had seen." [17]

Continuing beyond the confines of what are now the political boundaries of Peru, and into Ecuador and along the royal road, the same careful urban planning of cities continued.

Tumipampa (now called Tumibamba), and the place that is now the city of Cuenca, was ". . . built much like all the others," wrote Cieza in 1550. "On a large plain . . . near two small rivers . . . The Temple of the Sun is built of stones very cunningly wrought, some of them being large, coarse, and black, and others resembling jasper. Some of the Indians pretend that most of the stones of which these buildings and the Temple of the Sun are built had been brought from the great city of Cuzco . . . The doorways of many of the buildings were very handsome and brightly painted, with several precious gems and emeralds set into the stone, and the interior walls of the Temple of the Sun and of the palaces of the Incas were lined with plates of the finest gold stamped with many figures. The roofs were of straw so well put that no fire would consume it and it would endure for many ages. . . ."

The plan of the temple city included buildings with "more than two hundred virgins [who were very beautiful], dedicated to the service of the sun. Near the temples . . . were many buildings used as lodgings for the troops and as storehouses, which were always kept full." [65]

Quito, at the end of the Cuzco–Quito axis, three hundred miles from the Inca center at Tumibamba and 1,250 miles from Cuzco, was one of the large cities. Here, too—although Quito and its environs were not fully part of the empire until

1492—the Incas constructed their usual urban centers—and far in advance of anything Europe was doing at the same date. It was in full operation and "beautifully wrought" even within fifty years of its Inca conquest.

Architecturally we have now seen Inca centers picked at random and described along an approximate 2,000-mile-long stretch, from Lake Titicaca to Quito, at altitudes ranging between 8,500 and 13,000 feet. There are no other people in history who constructed and maintained such complex urban centers at such great heights.

As in the Andes, so with the coast: as they conquered the lands of the desert they modified the structures; when they had their victory, they leveled part of the old city and superimposed their plaza, Sun temples, and administrative center. When they built anew, they followed a formula almost exactly as had the Romans for their newly conquered territories. On the coast the Inca worked with adobe blocks; at important religious centers—such as the mecca of Pachacamac near Lima—stone was brought down and certain doorways and niches were constructed of it; adobe was used above the stone. At newly constructed sites such as Incahuasi in the Cañete Valley and Tambo Colorado in the adjoining valley of Pisco, the Inca masons worked only with adobe, but fashioned and shaped it as they would stone.

As the Greeks had their "key," and the Romans their eagle, so the Incas had their niche. The trapezoidal window (false or real) was the mark of the Inca; whenever an existing structure was modified, the architect added the niche. Nothing is so indicative as this; wherever it appears it marks the presence of these people.

Enough, then, has been shown of Inca structures along a wide and lengthy geography to show that we are dealing with a *master plan;* the sheer quantity of extant Inca structures, in whole or in part, is so utterly astonishing that no one has ever attempted to make a detailed account of the whole of it. However, the persistence of design throughout thousands of miles of varied terrain proves the point long insisted upon by an old Inca hand: "All the best-known monuments of *Inca* architecture were constructed not by individuals but by the government, according to careful plans." [53]

It is now time to see how the builders worked.

Many writers on these problems—and included therein are many archaeologists—take this position, that the cyclopean stonework which one sees in Cuzco and especially in the fortress of Sacsahuamán (one of the greatest single structures ever reared by ancient man) was pre-Inca, and all this stonework is attributed to some vague and shadowy anterior civilization called by them the "Megalithic empire." This position has little archaeological support. The varying styles, it has been abundantly shown by excavation and restoration, are only the evolution of Inca styles themselves, or what is more likely, the difference in building materials and the plasticity of the Inca craftsmen.

And of stone. When the gigantic size of the stones that form these structures is viewed for the first time, the utter enormity of the task of shaping, transporting them, and putting them into place—the edges so chamfered as to join without even a semblance of joining—is such that the viewer refuses to submit to the inescapable conclusion that the stone was quarried, pulled into place without draft animals, fashioned by stone instruments, and raised by crude leverage. Although such monoliths weighed as much as sixty tons and were variously shaped, they were made and fitted easily without cement, seemingly as a Chinese craftsman handles a piece of ivory. Such structures, except where destroyed by man, have resisted the insults of time for hundreds of years.

While working stone with stone celts seems to hinge on the marvelous, it is scarcely unique in history. Polished stone-celt instruments had a great significance for Neolithic man—before the introduction of metal—and great care was given to the making of stone instruments; axes, adzes, chisels, hammers, all appear in stone, and later metal ones are only a counterpart of stone instruments. The Incas, as well as the other cultures before them, had metal, even a hard bronze, but the stone celt remained their tool. The early Egyptians worked stone similarly. Metal, although it appeared in the Near East as early as 4000 B.C., *did not wholly replace stone celts until after 2000* B.C The sculptures in low relief that adorn the temples of Thebes in Egypt (dating circa 1500 B.C.) show Egyptian masons using stone implements almost identical in form and method of handling to the stone celt used by the Incas. Shaping stone with stone was universal and should occasion no surprise, nor is there the need of a fantastic explanation of how the Inca craftsman worked large rock masses.

Metal replaced stone celts very slowly in Eurasia, and it shows the slowness of the acceptance of new ideas that it took man (even when he had metal) two thousand years to replace stone instruments. It is not surprising, then, that the Incas, even with good bronze instruments, should continue to use stone celts. The advantages of metal should not be exaggerated in stoneworking; the Neolithic cultures showed clearly that trees could be felled, canoes shaped, posts made, and stone walls carved with stone instruments. Stone hammers were made from fine-grained heavier stone: hematite, basalt, or epidiorite. Stone chisels made of these materials are found abundantly in many Inca sites.

Quarrying of stone was done in America as the Egyptians and all other earlier cultures did it. Rock was searched for natural faults; after boring, the holes were filled with wooden wedges, swollen with water, and in time this swelling action cracked the huge rock masses. (The Romans, even with the most advanced technology of the ancient world, did it no differently.) Inca quarries are still to be seen on the mountain slopes opposite Ollantaytambo. There, at 1,500 feet above the river, are the quarries; stone, half-shaped, is still there. Rock shapes are partially formed out of the porphyritic rock, and the place is piled with rock chips. Quarries are also found at Huaccoto (black andesite), eight miles from Cuzco, and others at Rumicolca (*rumi*, "stone"), twenty-one miles from Cuzco, which yielded the fine rock reserved for the best of Inca structures. Limestone was used for the great fortress of Sacsahuamán, and it was fashioned into the enormous polygonal megaliths that form the base of the fortress. A study of the quarrying techniques of the Egyptians shows that they were almost identical with the techniques of the Incas.[59]

Transport of stone was by manpower. We can only deduce the transport techniques. Although the Indian did not have the wheel, he used wood and stone rollers, and the rock in the rough was pulled by ropes with manpower. He used levers operating on bosses, perhaps sledges for dragging, but had only the most elementary knowledge of dynamics and of methods for handling mass weight.

How were the buildings constructed? How was such intricate stonework (admittedly the finest ever done) worked without the tools we think necessary for such an operation? How the plans, the Incas having neither paper nor writing?

The Incas used clay models for buildings and terraces, even for town planning; some of these have survived in clay and stone. We have no knowledge of how the architect or mason measured. They had a crude slide rule and used a plumb bob (*wipayci*). Their standard for measurement is unknown. Doubtless, like the Egyptians, they used hands, feet, and other parts of the body for the basic measurements (the ancient Egyptian hieroglyph for the cubit was a forearm). We know that the spread of the human body became the measurement for the fathom. The Incas had a standard measurement for land. The standard width of a typical Inca road was about twenty-four feet, the spread of about five human Indian bodies; we know nothing beyond this.

This is admittedly not a wholly adequate explanation of how they attained the precision which they did. A study of the various stone styles displays their plasticity with stone, for the Inca craftsman had a long heritage in stoneworking. Some of the pre-Inca cultures, notably Tiahuanaco and those who built the beautiful round burial *chullpas* about Lake Titicaca five hundred years before the advent of the Incas, suggest this long inheritance. They had an aesthetic feeling for the *quality* of stone; this is only acquired after generations.

Stonework differed markedly in each structure according to its importance. The stones of the Temple of the Sun in Cuzco were squared and set with precision and made as smooth as marble; larger stones, on the temple of Inca Roca, were polygonal in style, showing a knowledge of thrust and strength by interlocking. How the Inca mason obtained this minute precision, in which the enormous stone had to be lifted and set down a hundred times before the massive rock fitted perfectly on all its sides like a bottle stopper, still cannot be satisfactorily explained.

Sacsahuamán was the great fortress, the *pucara* of Cuzco. It is without doubt one of the greatest structures ever erected by man. It was begun by Pachacuti ("Earthshaker") after A.D. 1438, and it employed thirty thousand Indians for the seventy years of its construction.[71] It was completed circa 1500; its fate was not unlike that of the Maginot line—it fell quickly. The principal fortifications face north; along this side is an unbroken wall over fifteen hundred feet in length. The cyclopean wall is composed of three massive tiers of stone walls, broken into forty-six parts, each supporting a terrace; the three parapets rising to a combined height of sixty feet are constructed of salients, retiring angles, and buttresses. There were only three doors—three entrances—and one of these still retains the name of the principal architect. There were two square military towers (*mayumarcas*) at either end of the front underground passages, an enormous water reservoir with stone-laid conduits in which the water passed from one place to another, a beautifully wrought palace for the Inca, storage places for food and arms, habitations for soldiers and people who would maintain the defense. The first Spaniards who saw it were speechless with astonishment ". . . neither the stone aqueduct of Segovia nor the buildings of Hercules nor the work of the Romans had the dignity of this fortress. . . ."[14]

How did they move the massive stones—some weighing

as much as twenty tons—into place and, even more, set these giant megaliths into place in such a way that the edges were chamfered where they joined and yet left the outer faces rough and even extended? First, the quarried stones were pulled on rollers. A pit was dug and the first stone was placed in it. The next stone, to be laid on top, was brought up by a ramp of pounded earth and stones (this method was seen by a Jesuit chronicler in the seventeenth century, and ramps are still found at the sites of some of the ruins). The protuberances one sees on the stones at Sacsahuamán were actually left there by the stonemason, to serve as a fulcrum to push the stone into place. As is obvious, the stone was brought unfinished; then it was cut so accurately it is impossible to push a knife blade between the stones. The immense rock masses remain to amaze us; Stonehenge pales beside it, the tomb of Agamemnon at Argos is as nothing alongside it; even the cyclopean wals of Agrigentum fall far short in comparison with the fortress of Sacsahuamán.

25 Metal and Metallurgy

ALTHOUGH GOLD, the old successful metal, was found in great quantities, the Incas in fact mined a considerable variety of other metals. Since copper, when mixed with tin, gave them bronze, it was the most important and was the only metal allowed to be used decoratively by the ordinary Indian.

The technology of metals was known, it seemed, to all the world's peoples. Historically the first metal to be mined was gold, for it made life sumptuous. Iron rusted, silver tarnished; gold was the metal of great ductility. Copper came next in man's metal age, then tin. Man's pattern in the New World was the same as in the Old.

Copper was mined in Mesopotamia as early as 3500 B.C., and it appears first in Peruvian graves sometime after 2000 B.C. The Incas, when they appeared, brought no new techniques, but they did organize the method of obtaining it. First, all the gold and silver mined and in mines belonged to the Inca. All bullion had to come to Cuzco; no Indian was allowed to leave the city with any of it on his person.

Mining, then as now, was disliked by the Indian. It took him from his land and, while gold might have its value, land was forever. Since gold and copper and silver came from the Andes, the metal-bearing hills were sacred. They were considered *huacas*, and the Indians prayed while they dug that the gods would yield the metal from the hills.

The Incas had precise laws for mining and miners. The mines were only allowed to be worked in the Andes during the four warmest months. Miners were rotated; no miner could go into the mining districts without his woman. In the perpendicular hills that surrounded the terribly humid lands of the Carabaya (east of Lake Titicaca in the Montaña), where the Inca got much of his gold, the hills are terraced for crops and the remains of gold-mining villages are still found there. Gold was mostly secured by panning; another method was to build a series of stone riffles across the bed of a river, and stones which held gold particles were collected after the rains. Smelting of the gold into ingots was done by bringing the gold to the furnaces atop lofty hills, called *huayras;* these furnaces, operated with charcoal and bellows, faced east into the wind of the trades and gave sufficient draft to obtain the high temperatures needed for melting.

The Inca metallurgists used all the techniques known to metal-working: casting, hammering, soldering, riveting, and *repoussé*. The goldsmiths (who were stationed within Cuzco itself and were exempt from taxes) used the techniques described by Garcilaso de la Vega, "the Inca," who was born in Cuzco in 1539 and no doubt saw them at their bellows and blast furnaces: "they went round the fire blowing with the tubes."

This technique is no different from that depicted on a Egyptian tomb at Saqqara (dating back to 2400 B.C.), where goldsmiths can be seen blowing into a fire to create the heat needed to melt gold. From this relatively crude method came the Inca gold pieces which so astonished the Spaniards, such a golden torrent that the captured Lord-Inca Atahualpa could fill a vast room twice with silver and once with gold images torn from the walls and interiors of his empire; and all within the space of six months. From these crude methods they were able to cast life-size figures of Incas, and the golden mimicry of plant life found in the Golden Enclosure at Cuzco.

Gold, of course, is highly ductile; it is softer than silver —a single grain of it can be drawn into a wire a hundred feet long—and it is universal in appeal. Gold roads are found in many parts of the ancient world, and ancient peoples knew more about gold than any other metal. The Egyptians had a papyrus map dated 1300 B.C. which showed where gold mines were located. The Incas, too, had detailed statistics on gold. There were officials at the mines to check on production and miners, but whereas in other lands miners were usually criminals, among the Incas it was carried on by the people as part of their work tax.

Gold belonged to the Inca. No one knows how much gold the empire produced, yet from the accurate *quipu* records which were interpreted to the Spaniards it was believed that gold came into Cuzco at the rate of seven million ounces annually.

After his death, each of the Lord-Incas had a life-sized gold statue (*pucarina*) made of him, and his palace, which became his tomb, was ornamented with gold.

Silver, too, was the Inca's divine property. Silver was a quality rather than a substance, and the tender moonlight luster of its brilliance caused the Indians to regard it as the tears of the moon. It was plenteous in Peru. All people at all times have loved the elegance, the elegy of silver; Sanskrit poems are full of images of silver bells; the Greeks who went as far as the Volga River for trade, found silver mines being worked there by the primitive Scythians. And even though silver tarnished easily in the humidity of the Andes, the

Incas regarded it highly; much of the metalwork in Cuzco was of silver. Quicksilver, too, was known to the Incas; there is a large mine at Huancavelica, worked by the Spaniards for centuries; it was no doubt used in the gold- and silver-plating of bronze, a technique used by the Inca smiths to "extend" the quantity of gold. The techniques of Peruvian metallurgy have not been extensively studied. However, we know they used tin alloys, and tin is found in much of what appears at first sight to be pure gold; they employed a formula for combining copper and tin to produce bronze, casting them in one piece and hammering it cold. With such casting techniques they produced maceheads for war clubs, hard bronze levers (*chumpis*), knives (*tumis*), a fairly diverse list of surgical instruments, bolas used for the ensnaring of birds and animals, pins (*topos*) to hold the women's garments together, ear spoons and hair tweezers; the list could be

39. *Figure of a woman cast in silver. Although this is only eight inches in height, the conquistadors reported they found life-sized figures of cast gold and silver.*

extended, yet it is enough to display the wide application of metallurgy. All of it was overshadowed, of course, by the immense amount of gold and silver ornaments.

What this golden flow amounted to in terms of bullion

value and purchase value has been shown by Dr. Samuel K. Lothrop.[38] The gold and silver which was collected at Caja-marca, brought there by the orders of the Lord-Inca Atahualpa who was held captive by the Spaniards and who agreed to ransom himself by filling a room twenty-five feet long and fifteen feet wide "as high as a white line which a tall man could not reach," amounted to 1,326,539 pesos of pure gold and 51,610 marks of silver.* This amounted, in terms of actual value of bullion (at $35.02 the ounce), to $19,851,-642.00. In purchasing value this sum would be at present worth ten times that amount. The Inca hoard of gold and silver is put forward in terms of bullion value only to give some idea of the enormous amount of it; in terms of art, the value of these objects is incalculable. Naturally, to be transportable and divisible among the conquistadors, these art objects had to be melted down and put into ingots. Although some of the remarkable pieces of goldwork were set aside for the Emperor Charles V of Spain, *not a single object of art survived;* all of it went into the crucibles by reason of a royal edict (February 13, 1535): "All gold and silver from Peru shall be melted in the royal mints at Sevilla, Toledo and Segovia."

All we know of this lost art is what the common soldier, touched by what he saw, wrote about these fantastic pieces of goldsmithery, many worthy of a Benvenuto Cellini. "In Cuzco . . . they found many statues and images entirely of gold and silver, complete shape of a woman *in natural size* very well wrought, well shaped and hollow; these I believe were the finest that could be made anywhere. . . ." Another conquistador wrote of seeing "many vessels of gold, lobsters of the sort that grow in the sea and on other gold vessels were sculptured with all birds and serpents, even spiders, lizards and sort of beetles . . . carved on the body of gold." And the conquistador's secretary, who recorded all of the booty before it was consigned to the goldsmiths who melted it down into ingots, saw it all piled high: "Truly it was a thing worthy to be seen . . . vessels, vases and pieces of various forms in which the [Inca] lords of the land were served . . . there were four llamas in fine gold and very large, ten or twelve figures of women, natural size, all of fine gold and as beautiful and well made it seemed as if they were alive. . . ."

* Lothrop gives the complicated methods of determining gold and silver weights in the sixteenth century, mark = 230.675 grams; peso de oro = 4.18 grams.

26 Tawantinsuyu: The Four Quarters of the World

FROM CUZCO (as from Rome, with imperial ways) issued the great roads which ran the length and breadth of the empire. The center point from which all the roads issued was the great square of Cuzco, Huaycapata, around which stood the principal buildings of the realm. Here the people met, their voices in jarring contention, and had their fetes, days of merrymaking that broke the monotony of their lives.

The great square was also the demarcation for the four great quarters, or *suyus,* of the world into which the Inca realm was divided. The sum of those parts made up Tawantin-suyu, the official name of the empire.

Neither the four quarters nor the roads conformed exactly to the direction of the four cardinal points of the compass. Rather the boundaries were fixed by the conformation of the geography of the land. Each *suyu* was ruled by a governor (*apo*), of royal lineage and related by blood ties to the Inca; he was answerable only to the Inca.

Cuzco, although in the heartland of the Andes, actually lies very close to the jungles of the Upper Amazon. It is only scant miles from the upper Urubamba River; four days of an Indian's walk northeast would carry him into the jungles. And directly east, two days' walk would bring an Indian to the Paucartambo, a gigantic river which cascades mile upon mile down into a jungle of towering trees and constant rainfall. Here a bewildering number of fierce tribesmen, "untamed" Indians, who, with the consistency of ants, were never discouraged by devastating setbacks, kept hacking at the outposts of the Inca's realm. Three of the empire's most gigantic fortresses—Sacsahuamán, which guarded holy Cuzco itself, Ollantaytambo, twenty-four miles northwest of Cuzco (which defended the upper Urubamba River, a natural gateway to Cuzco), and Pisac, another gigantic fortress, which guarded the upper reaches of the same river as well as the pass which led east to Paucartambo—were erected to guard against the incursions of the jungle tribes into the environs of Cuzco.

The whole of this quarter was the Antisuyu. It is difficult

to be precise about what the quarter covered. Presumably all land east of the Andes, where the trees began—the eyebrows of the forest, as the Spaniards had it—fell under the administration of the governor of the Antisuyu. It was immense. The Inca seemed to lump all the people under the name of *yungas* or hotland people; actually they were very diverse, and ranged from those who wore woolen ponchos and lived mostly off a tuber called manioc, to the half-naked Indians in the hotlands of the Amazon. Stone-paved roads were pushed into the very jungle itself, garrisons were kept up at full war strength, and the Inca himself, in the later days of the reign, was engaged constantly in repulsing attacks from that quarter.

The Incas were able, in some instances, to win over the tribes here, and they yielded tribute in the form of gold, bird feathers, *chonta* wood, dyes, fruits, animal skins, wood fibers, and jungle-reared cotton. Other tribes, notably the Aguarunas ("water people"), a subtribe of the head-hunting Shuaras, never yielded, and the Inca's troops were decimated in the humid jungles where the tactics of mass attack and envelopment were of little value. Most of these jungle Indians knew of copper and bronze instruments, which they had through trade with the Incas. Each quarter had its official royal *tampu*, or way station, approximately thirty miles from Cuzco; the administrative post of the Antisuyu quarter was Paucartambo.

The next quarter, in the exact opposite direction from Cuzco, was the Cuntisuyu. It lay southwest of Cuzco, and was reached by a road (still to be seen in parts) which led over the Andes. The administrative *tampu*, approximately twenty-one miles from Cuzco, was Paccari-tampu (called "Origin Tampu," and believed to have been one of the places where the first Incas emerged to begin the wars that led to their capture of the Cuzco Valley).

Cuntisuyu is not clearly defined, but conforming to the Inca concepts of geography it embraced all the land lying between Cuzco and the Pacific Ocean and south as far as what is now the Peru-Chile border, and north to, and perhaps beyond, where modern Lima now stands. It took in the high bleak Andean lands, and also the great tribal cultures that lived on the Peruvian desert littoral, those which we now call the Nazca, Ica, Chanca, etc., as well as the famous shrine of Pachacamac, the mecca of the creator-god.

For one hundred years the Incas made war upon the coastal tribes who lived in this quarter, and lateral roads, wonderfully built, were made to cling to the sides of the gorges of the rivers which ran west; almost every valley had such roads. War occupied the affairs of the *apo* or governor of this quarter until about 1466, when the Incas finally conquered the Chimú Empire. This effectively ended all opposition on the coast.

This administrative post was very important. It involved winning the conquered people over to the Inca system and organizing their tribute, resettling "safe populations" (referred to as *mitimaes*) among them, and setting up the royal *tampus* along the roads so as to bring to Cuzco the coastal products: cotton, dyestuffs, food (peanuts, manioc, sweet potatoes, squash, etc.), and especially fresh fish and seaweed (of considerable importance to the Inca diet), which had to be brought by running relays.

The third quarter was the Collasuyu. In size of territory it was the largest of the four, and lay to the southeast. The road to it went out from the small plaza in Cuzco still known by its Quechua name Rimacpampa. This quarter embraced all the land southeast of Cuzco, including Lake Titicaca, what is now Bolivia, Chile (except its very humid tip), and the whole of mountainous Argentina. The governor of this *suyu*, after the conquests won it for the Inca realm, had to balance his administration between severe reprisals and the winning arts of diplomacy, for here were the Aymara-speaking peoples, once as great in numbers as the Quechua-speaking peoples. They still lived in the aura of the past greatness of Tiahuanaco, whose ruins, lying at the edge of Lake Titicaca, were always there to give evidence that the Incas had arrived late and were not the Sun God-inspired people that they claimed to be. There was gold from the Carabaya, vicuña and alpaca wool from the high places, tin and copper from Bolivia to make bronze, and ostrich feathers from the pampas.

The fourth and last quarter was Chinchasuyu. Its royal *tampu* and administrative center was Rimacpampa, some thirty-six miles from Cuzco near the banks of the Apurimac River. Its direction was northwest and its administration included all the Andean area between Cuzco and Quito, a distance of 1,250 miles. The immense quarter was named after a lake, Chinchaycocha (now Junín) the second largest in South America after Titicaca, which lies more or less in the geographical center of Peru. The Chinchay had tribes who fought long and valiantly against the Inca, but when finally subdued they became loyal vassals.

All of the important later conquests of the Incas took place within this last section, and from it many of the great arterial roads struck off for conquests of the desert coast and the Upper Amazon. As a symbol of this great quarter the Inca selected tribes, keeping them to their dress and customs, and set them at Karmenka, at the "gateway" to Cuzco on the road to Chinchasuyu. Here lived the Cañari and the Chacha-poya tribesmen.

The posts of governors (*apos*)—Incas of royal blood—were hereditary; they ruled their quarters from Cuzco or from the administration center of each royal *tampu* located thirty miles from Cuzco in each direction. Statistical records were kept in each quarter by means of the *quipu* knot-string records. These arrived with each post by *chasquis* (couriers) who came bearing messages in this form; they were then translated

40. *The* quipu, *as redrawn from the Inca-Spanish chronicler, Poma de Ayala. The domino-like figure to the left suggests the manner in which its decimal system of counting should be understood.*

into decimal figures by the *quipu* readers (*quipu-camayoc*) and transmitted to the governor. Thus he would know how many taxpayers (able-bodied Indians) lived in his quarter, the number of llamas in the herds, the exact number of soldiers he could call at a moment's notice, the cities, and the royal stopping places that lay within his jurisdiction. At any imperial council, also a hereditary post, he could give this information to the Inca. Since we do not have any exact figures of the number of Indians in the Inca realm at the time of the Spanish conquest, we do not know how many people each governor of a given *suyu* controlled. Various population figures have been given—six million, one of the "accepted" numbers, seems far too large; two million is perhaps more in line. With this as a hypothetical figure then, each governor would control 500,000 people. The next chieftain was a *hono-curaca,* who controlled 10,000 people; under him, a *pica-waranka-curaca,* who controlled 5,000 Indians, and so it went down the line until the very last, the "straw boss," a *cancha-camayoc,* responsible for ten Indians. For every 10,000 Indians there were 1,331 officials. Everything was based on head count; all was decimally organized.

The Inca's orders, as Dr. Wendell Bennett sagely observed, "flowed up and orders flowed down, but there was little communication between officers of the same rank." This was to cause problems later.

Certain of the quarters provided their specialists; from the Cuntisuyu quarter came the Rucana tribe, a rugged high-dwelling people who were used to the perpendicular world. They were the official litter-bearers; eighty of them, in a special blue livery, were assigned to each royal litter. The Chumpivilcas tribesmen from another quarter were the dancers, and the Chichas supplied the incense for the religion of the Sun. There were others who were distinctly professionals: architects, professional soldiers, accountants (*quipu-camayoc*), silversmiths (*kolki-camayoc*), tapestry weavers (*kumpi-camayoc*), and this again suggests how well defined was the organization.

Women within the four quarters were, as were their menfolk, fully controlled. They were subject to a head count, and all girls above ten years of age were classified. Young girls who possessed beauty, grace, or talent were brought to the attention of the visiting *curacas,* signaled out, and brought to Cuzco to become Chosen Women. Those not selected were known as "left-out girls." The Chosen Women were placed under supervision (they might be likened to nuns), trained to weave, and were attached to the rituals attending the religion of the Sun. Those so trained were "Handmaidens of the Sun," and were established throughout the empire wherever there were Sun temples. Their dwelling places, out of reach of ordinary men, were placed high in some inaccessible spot, such as one can still see at the ruins of Ollantay-tambo or at Incahuasi (New Cuzco) in the Cañete Valley.

There were as many as fifteen thousand such Chosen Women, and those who were not connected with the rituals pertaining to the Sun were either taken in royal concubinage or else as wives by famous generals. Later, if unmarried, the Chosen Women assumed the titles of *mamacuna* and became the instructresses of the newly arrived Chosen Women. They wove garments exclusively for the use of the Lord-Inca and his *coya*.

It was these women, quartered at Caxas in the Sun Temple in northern Peru, that the Spanish soldiers raped in the first five days of the conquest. This so enraged the Inca that he planned their annihilation, which only his capture prevented.*

The four quarters of the Inca realm were constantly being enlarged, and territorial expansion gave the Incas a new social world with an "intensified horizontal and vertical social mobility. The need for administrators was so urgent that any man, no matter how humble his origin, who showed the slightest spark of administrative ability might find himself set down in a strange village miles from his home and told to enforce the emperor's law." [53]

The *apo* governors knew no rest from their labors. Since conquest with the Incas constituted the growth of empire, administration was bound up with colonization. Upon conquering a new area, perhaps an alien tribe, the governor of the quarter in which the conquest took place had one of several policies to follow. If the tribe had yielded gracefully, even after furious battle, the conquered chiefs were allowed to retain their titles (although they remained under the dominance of the Inca governor), and their sons, as aforementioned, were sent to Cuzco for training and held as hostages for the good behavior of the chieftains. Conquered peoples were allowed their local dress; in fact this was insisted upon, and up to a certain point they retained their own speech, although all the officials had to learn Quechua if they did not know it already. All had to observe the religion of the Sun. If their local gods were efficacious, if they had a well-known *huaca* within their territory, the gods were adopted into the Inca pantheon.

---

* These were the Chosen Women that the first Spaniards mass-raped at the mountain village of Caxas. They forced five hundred Virgins of the Sun out into the plaza, and while crossbowmen kept off any Indians, the soldiers had their way with them until worn out and spent; they went off then and continued the conquest. Later, when he met them at Cajamarca, the Inca charged the Spaniards with this as a heinous crime.

However, if the conquered tribe was recalcitrant and refused to accept the Inca's ways, they were decimated, or if too large, they were moved out of their own lands and a reliable, "safe" Quechua-speaking people were put into the voided land. These *mitimaes* played the same role in the newly conquered quarter as the Roman soldier had played in his conquests. Their mission was to teach Inca cultural ways, so they were in their way the "civilizers."

The administration of so far-flung an empire depended on its communications, and as the great plaza of Cuzco was the demarcation of its four sections, so too was the plaza the starting point of its roads—the web of communications which bound the realm together.

27 The Royal Roads of the Incas

THERE WERE historically only two road systems: the Roman roads, which covered fifty-six thousand linear miles through Europe, the Near East, and Africa, and that of the Incas, which moved across the surface of the Andes from Argentina to Colombia and along the entire length of desert coast, amounting to more than ten thousand miles ofm all-weather highways.

In order to hold the Inca realm together and to convert these congeries of geography—desert, mountain, and jungle —into a close-knit empire, the best of communications was needed; the result was the Inca road, a system only comparable to the Roman roads, an American labor which Alexander von Humboldt (who knew both) characterized as "the most useful and stupendous works ever executed by man."

In the main there were two sections of roads; the royal road (*Capacñan*), which moved through the Andes from the border of the empire at the Ancasmayo River (1° N. lat.), down through Ecuador, Peru, Bolivia, and thereafter into Argentina (coming to an end at Tucumán), and then into Chile, where it ended at the Rio Maule (35° S. lat.). There the Incas built a fortress and their most southern station at Purumauca. The coastal road, beginning at Tumbes (3° S. lat.), the frontier city which marked the coastal end of the Inca realm, ran southward through the brazen desert, the entire length of Peru; thence down deep into Chile, connecting at Copiapó with the road coming over from Argentina and continuing down to the Maule in Chile, which marked its end.

The Andean royal road was 3,250 miles in length (making it longer than the longest Roman road—from Hadrian's Wall in Scotland to Jerusalem); the coastal road was 2,520 miles in length.

In addition to these arterial roads, there were numerous laterals, careening down the sides of the V-shaped valleys and connecting the mountain roads with the coastal one; there were special gold roads, such as those which moved into the rich gold areas of Carabaya, east of Lake Titicaca, and there were especially wide military roads such as the one built from Huánuco to Chachapoyas, stone-laid in its entire length of

161

four hundred miles in order to undertake the conquest of an escaped tribe of Chanca Indians. Roads also pervaded the jungle. They were built at the highest altitudes ever used by man in constant travel; the highest Inca road recorded (17,160 feet) is the one behind Mount Salcantay.

The standard width of the Inca coastal road was twenty-four feet. It is not known, as yet, why so wide a standard was set or what precise measurement determined it, but from hundreds of measurements made upon the road by the von Hagen Expedition along one thousand miles, this was the standard gauge; [72] it only departed from it when some immovable obstacle prevented this "official" width from being obtained. Considerable nonsense has been written about the roads: to some they were mere footpaths, and to others stone roads laid with porphyry; neither extreme is true. The Incas had no wheel and no draft animals; the common denominators were the foot of the Indian and the hoof of the llama. There was no need for the deep roadbed of the Roman roads which were solidly constructed to accommodate vehicular traffic. And it is known historically that *nowhere did prepared surfaces appear on ancient roads* until wheeled transport came into general use.

On the coast the natural hard-packed surfaces of the coastal llanos were sufficiently hard to support traffic without a surface. When the road passed over a bog it was raised high like a causeway; when it moved down steep inclines it became a step road. When the roads entered the larger coastal cities and their environs, they were often paved for short distances.

The consistent twenty-four-foot width is the architectural feature which distinguishes the Inca roads from those built by anterior civilizations. Another feature of the Inca road is the side wall to keep out the sand drift, to mark the road, and to keep the soldiers, who mostly used it, within the bounds of the road. This was one of the first things noted by the Spaniards. "Along this coast and vales the Caciques and prime men made a road . . . with strong Walls on both sides. . . ." [14] These walls can still be seen in many places marching across the naked desert, which is devoid of everything else save this remarkable road.

The road was marked along its entire length by *topos* (road markers), "with the distance between them," said Cieza de León, who interested himself in such things, "a Castillian league and a half," i.e., 4½ miles. (The Romans, it will be recalled, put up road markers computing the distances in number of miles from the Forum in Rome; more than four thousand have been found.)

There is always a reason behind communications; the Assyrians had roads for conquest, and they built one "making it shine like the light of day"; Darius the Persian built a royal road of stone between Susa and Babylonia, which Herodotus knew; it, too, had stone mile markers. All roads of any length have always been royal roads and have always had distances marked. There is a line of logic which appears in the road story: all land armies, bound on conquest, had to have roads. Rome was such a state, the Incas were such a people; both had good roads.

The coastal road, twenty-four feet wide along its length of 2,520 miles, was connected by lateral roads with the royal road in the Andes. Eleven such laterals have been explored, but there are doubtless many more. Every valley of consequence had these lateral communications. Many were pre-Inca roads (not as well engineered and lacking the overall master plan of width and construction) and these the Inca engineers either disregarded or else in time-honored fashion built theirs on top of the older ones. At first these were Inca conquest roads, brought down from the Andes into various valleys to overwhelm the enemy by mass attack. One lateral, typical of all of them and the best preserved, is that road which connects the two arterial roads through the valley of Cañete. The Incas had built New Cuzco (now called Incahuasi), the largest coastal structure there, and their road alongside it. They preferred to build their road against the canyon walls; it was chipped away, terraced, and the sides built up with dry-laid stone. Drainage, when the roads reached the wet zone, was important, and it was provided for every rivulet, for here streams and rivers shift their banks with callous ease. They excluded water, that wanton destroyer of communications, completely from their roads. They dealt with water as the Romans did: they outwitted it by making sure that it was not there. This particular Cañete Valley lateral moved up from sea level across and up over a land height of 15,600 feet, stone-paved a good portion of the way, to emerge 125 miles beyond in the valley of Jauja (a great Inca center in the later days of the realm); there it became connected with the royal road of the Andes.

The 3,250-mile-long road commenced beyond Quito, close to the natural bridge across the Ancasmayo river (now Colombia), made its way down the Andean valleys, then over the treeless *puna,* and, as has already been described, moved down toward South America's southern tip. This was, until the nineteenth century, the longest arterial road of history. Its width varies between fifteen and eighteen feet, suggesting that either the coastal twenty-four-foot road was a later development or that the Andean road was a compromise with geography; it was difficult to maintain so wide a road except under unusual circumstances in this perpendicular land. Like its coastal counterpart, it was unpaved except where there was unavoidable water; then it was made into a causeway as at Anta, near to Cuzco, built circa A.D. 1300. It is twenty-four feet wide and *eight miles long* and stands eight feet above the wide-spreading quagmire; it is more or less as Pedro de Cieza de León saw it in 1549, a "great swamp which could only be crossed with difficulty, had the Inca not built a wide-paved causeway."

There are other engineering feats to be seen elsewhere on this long road.

It is not possible to give an exact date for the construction of these roads. All anterior Peruvian cultures had roads. There were those built by the Mochicas, Tiahuanacans, and Chimús, the techniques of which were taken over by the Incas. But as the Romans, so the Incas. In Rome it was the highest honor to build a road and have it carry one's name; Gaius Caesar personally laid down stretches of Roman road, and the Claudian family defrayed expenses for the roads when public funds were not available. The Incas were justly proud of their *Capac-ñan;* many of the names of the reigning Incas are connected with a particular road.

In Peru, to show the logic behind the road of any imperial people (who, landbound, acted similarly), the 2,500-mile road that joined Cuzco to Chile was known as the *Huayna Capacñan,* named after one of the last Incas (died 1527). Often an Inca would build a road wider and longer than his predecessors.

And how were they built? "I will explain," wrote Cieza de León in 1550, "the ease with which they were constructed by the Indians without increasing the death rate or causing excessive labor. When the Inca decided to have one of these famous roads constructed much preparation was unnecessary; it remained but for the Inca to give orders. For then the overseers [i.e., professional roadbuilders] went over the ground, made the trace of the road, and the Indians received instructions to construct the road using local labor. Each province completed the section of the road within its own limits; when it reached the end of their boundary [*ayllu*], it was taken up by others; when it was urgent, all worked at the same time."

It was evident that the builders were instructed from a master plan; the engineering of the bridges, the step road, constructed when perpendicular mountains were to be crossed, drainage, and terracing show general uniformity throughout this long stretch of road.

Although the road was wide, it was not designed for vehicular traffic, and it is very doubtful that, without draft animals, and in this upside-down land, it would have done them much good, even if they had had the wheel. This type of terrain was not fitted, in the mountains at least, for wheeled traffic. Then, why so wide a road?

The empire, for economical reasons, did not need so elaborate a network of roads since most of the provinces had considerable economic independence; for the north-south axis such a road designed for pure commerce was superfluous. In the main they were roads of conquest. Once a territory was conquered, the roads were important for control over

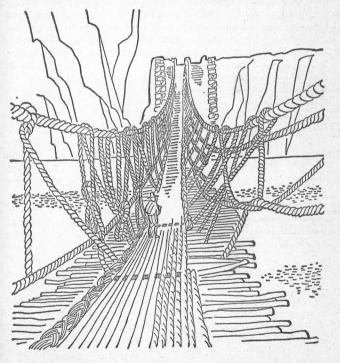

41. *The Apurimac* chaca—*the bridge that crossed the Apurimac River. Known in literature as* The Bridge of San Luis Rey. *It was one of the greatest engineering feats of the Incas. Although the fiber cables had to be changed every two years, the bridge survived from 1350 until 1890. Drawn from a daguerreotype taken by E. George Squier in 1865.*

the newly annexed territory. Prescott was correct when he wrote: "Not an insurrectionary movement could occur, not an invasion on the remotest frontier, before the tidings were conveyed to the capital and the imperial armies were on the march across the magnificent roads to suppress it. . . ."

Since the object of battle was to win, roads were built to get the warriors into battle in the fastest possible time. This was the *reason* for the Inca's roads.

On the high places along the road, the Incas, following ancient customs, placed *apachetas* (*apa*, "burden," *cheta*, "depositor"). Still to be seen in some places, they were propitiatory cairns formed of small rocks of about hand size. As travelers passed along the road, heavily laden, they placed a stone on the *apacheta* as a symbol of the burden, "and so they left their tiredness behind." [21] The road feature, which has nothing to do with engineering, is mentioned because the Persians did the same along their roads: ". . . Darius came to another river, the Artiscus . . . here he indicated a certain spot where every man in the army was ordered to deposit a stone as he passed by. This was done with the result that when Darius moved on he left great hills of stones behind him." Thus Herodotus.

28 Bridges

THE BRIDGE, an integral development of the road, and the little brother of the road, was one of the proudest of Inca achievements. So sacred the bridge that death was decreed for any who tampered with one.

42. *Hanging bridge over the Rio Pampas. Redrawn from E. George Squier, Peru, 1877.*

There were many types of bridges: suspension, pontoon, cantilever; clapper types (for crossing small streams), permanent and of stone slabs. All had their special names, but the generic name for bridge was *chaca*. The greatest of these *chacas* was the one that crossed the formidable gorge and

river of the Apurimac. It has entered literary immortality as
The Bridge of San Luis Rey; it was the greatest and without
doubt the most outstanding example of native engineering
known in the Americas.

When the Incas broke out of the traditional territory that
was Inca, they first had to bridge the Apurimac River in
order to be able to move northward. This occurred circa
A.D. 1350 and the bridge was built by the Lord-Inca Roca.

To describe it (since it was carefully studied by the von
Hagen Expedition) [72] is to describe most of the bridges of
this type (of which more than forty large ones, and no less
than a hundred smaller ones, bridged the chasms along the
route of the royal roads of the Incas).

The limitations: the Andean Indians had no wood readily
available; they did not know the arch; they knew and often
used the cantilever type of bridge, as for the stone bridge of
Carabaya (see Plate VIII), but this could only be used to
bridge rivers not much more than forty feet in width; so
without arch or wood, they perfected the suspension bridge.
They reversed the arch through suspension cables, for depending as it does on the principles of gravity, pressure, and
weight, the arch is earthbound and passive. The Incas reversed the arch curve and gave it wings—and it became the
hanging bridge. First in construction—the cables; those of
this particular bridge were accurately measured by an American in 1864; they were 148 feet long (add an additional
forty feet for imbedding). They were as thick as a man's
body, plaited and twisted as rope cables are, made in fact
from the same material as modern rope is—the *cabuya* (a
plant related to the *agave,* the fleshy-leaved century plant).
The cables were spun at the edge of the river to be bridged
(it was the technique of spinning steel cables at the place of
construction that John Roebling introduced for the first time
in the building of the Brooklyn Bridge), and then the cables
were brought across to the other side. They were then buried
deep in the earth and held by six wooden beams ("as thick
as oxen" says Garcilaso "the Inca"), then raised onto tall
stone pillars which supported the cables. The action was
repeated on the other side. Three other cables, tied to the
base of the stone towers, formed the "floor" of the bridge, the
suspension cables and the floor cables were then held together
by additional cables and the floor of the bridge had wooden
supports (see Figures 41 and 42). The middle of the bridge
sagged from its own weight, and there were no guy ropes
added to steady the bridge so that in the high winds it
swayed dangerously.

The Apurimac bridge was known as the *huaca chaca.* The

43. *The overseer of the bridges, as redrawn from Felipe Guamán Poma de Ayala circa 1565. The first illustration ever made of an Inca bridge. It is a good representation of the stone structures built to hold the fiber suspension cables.*

early Spaniards crossed it with fright and terror, and their letters are filled with their plaints about it. Yet to the Incas crossing it was no problem. They were not mounted and their llamas did not seem to share the fright of white man's mules.

This bridge, built circa A.D. 1350, endured for over five hundred years; it lasted through the entire Inca regime, was kept up by the Spaniards during the entire colonial epoch (ended 1824), and it continued in use during the republican government. The bridge was finally abandoned about 1890.

Suspension cables were renewed every year. The village of Curahuasi, eighteen miles north, had as part of its *mita* the job of upkeep of the bridge (and it was so traditional that the villagers kept this up until the bridge fell into disuse). This was equally true of all bridges of this type in the Inca realm; the village closest to it was expected to keep it up. At many places along the road there were two suspension bridges, hanging side by side—one for the higher men, the other for the lower, who paid tolls to cross it. Hernando Pizarro, on his march to the coast from the Andes to hurry up the flow of gold for the Inca's ransom, first described an Inca bridge on January 14, 1533, after coming down the step road to Piga, where they came to a canyon (Santa River): "It was spanned by two bridges close together made of network . . . They build a foundation near the water and raise it to a great height, and from one side of the river to the other there are cables . . . thick as a man's thigh. By one of these bridges the common people cross over and a guard *is stationed to receive transit dues* [italics added]." Later on, during their return over another road, at the great city of Huánuco they crossed another bridge, "over a torrential river [the Vizcarro] made of three thick logs and where *there are guards who collect a toll as is customary among these Indians* [italics added]."

44. *Totora balsa bridge over the outlet of Lake Titicaca. Redrawn from E. George Squier, Peru, 1877.*

Permanent bridges of stone or of wood were used over small streams (many are still to be seen), and where minor traffic did not justify labor expenditure, there was another

type, called *oroya*, two cables stretched between stone towers, with a basket attached to one of the cables and drawn
to either side by means of additional ropes.

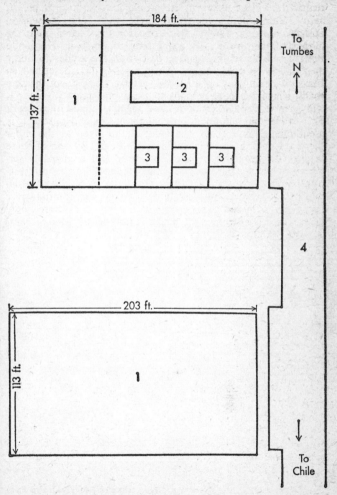

45. *The form and functions of* tampus, *Inca way stations. The ground
plan of the costal* tampu *at Saña.*
1) Presumably night stalls for llamas. 2) Areas for soldiers or travelers
along the road. 3) Individual rooms. 4) The 24-foot-wide coastal
road. Drawn by Pablo Carrera from the notes of the author.

The final bridge type, which also struck the first Spaniards as ingenious, was the balsa pontoon bridge. The most notable was the one that crossed the only river that drains Lake Titicaca. These were built as all pontoon bridges, except that here the pontoons were balsas, straw boats made of *totora* grass. These craft (see Transport, page 177) were placed side by side, linked by a thick cable, which in turn was held by stone towers on the opposite shore; a grass floor was laid over the grass balsa boats. As this type of grass boat becomes water-logged, the pontoons were replaced every two years; it was the duty of the village of Chacamarca ("Bridge Village") to replace these as part of their *mita* (labor tax). This bridge endured for over eight hundred years; it was used until 1875.

29 *The* Tampu *Stations*

TWO NECESSARY functions make a road: one is maintenance (for without it, as the African natives say, "the road dies"); the other is accommodation. All of those historical empires that built roads, Persian, Chinese, or Roman, had a system of post-houses for the accommodation of travelers. The Persians maintained theirs approximately eighteen miles apart, Herodotus affirms, ". . . at intervals along the road are recognized stations with excellent inns . . . over a distance of 94½ *parsangs* [about 330 miles] there are twenty stations . . . and the total of stations or post-houses on the road from Sardis to Susa is 111 . . ."

Along the sides of the Chinese roads, built by the Chou Dynasty (circa 1150 B.C.), the way was spotted with khans along the desert, mountain, and plain; along the imperial highways of the Romans there were *mansiones,* night quarters. One traveled this road without prerogatives or penalties, and one could even purchase an *Itinerari Maritimi* which gave the distances between way stations and the positions of posthouses.

The Inca was also such an empire. They had a system of posthouses, and they were called *tampus:* ". . . . there were buildings and storehouses," wrote Pedro de Cieza de León who traveled between 1547 and 1550 along the entire royal road, "at every four-six leagues [twelve to eighteen miles], with great abundance of all provisions that the surrounding districts could supply . . . the overseers [*curacas*] who resided at the chief stations in the provinces took special care that the natives kept these *tampus* well provisioned."

Tampus were official. Since no one moved on the roads without permission, it follows that they could only use the way stations as part of their official journey. The distances between them depended on the terrain; in the mountains, if the going was perpendicular, they were twelve miles apart, a convenient day's journey upward; if on level ground, eighteen miles apart; if in the desert, the distance between water (for here water decides everything).

They were utilitarian, and so were built of rough field stone or adobe. Some of them consisted of a single large structure, 100 by 300 feet, others had a series of smaller

173

TANBOS

Ocaxamarca

ciudad y mezon vreal adonde estagua atagua pay
gaa donselepredero y amataro donfrad pizarro
san migel pueblo tanbo vreal _____

caxapampa pueblo tanbo vreal _____
guamachuco pueblo tanbo vreal y casas de guaynaua
pac ynga _____
tanbillo _____
tanbonuebo pueblo tanbovreal _____

con choco uillatanborre

al yminas de plata mezon vreal _____
ciudas pueblo tanbovreal _____
quiropampa tanbillo _____
piscopampa pueblo tanbovreal _____
guancabamba pueblo tanbo vreal _____
guaxi pueblo tanbo vreal y casas deguayna capaynga
pincos tanbo vreal _____
quinua tanbillo _____
toparaco tanbo vreal _____
guanocobiexo y los banos tanbillo casas de topayn
ga yupangui p deguaynacapacynga _____
kinsucancha tanbo vreal _____
ancas mayo tanbo vreal _____
uorau tanbo vreal _____
bombom tanbovreal puentedecrisnexas delyn
ga topaynga yupanqui _____
ninacaca pueblo tanbovreal _____
chinchaycocha pueblo tanbovreal _____
tarma pueblo tanbovreal _____

                                                ves de

46. List of tambos (tampus) along the entire Inca highway as given by
Felipe Guamán Poma de Ayala. The orthography is Spanish, but the text
is Quechua mixed with Spanish. The symbols indicate the type of tampu
at each stopping place.

rooms opening on a larger corral where the llamas were kept. On the coast, particularly at Chala in southern Peru in the midst of the sun-drenched desert, there were a series of small rooms with stone-lined underground storage chambers.

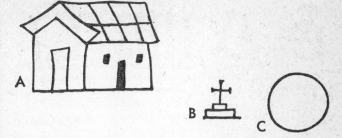

47. *The symbols of the three different types of* tampus *as listed by Felipe Guamán Poma de Ayala (see Figure* 46).
A) Royal *tampus* represented by a house. B) Lesser *tampus* for ordinary Indians. C) Auxiliary halting places represented by a circle.

Tampus were kept up by the local *ayllu* as part of its labor tax; each community was expected to see that the road approaching its section was in constant repair (women spun their wool as they walked so the roads had to be well metaled), and that the *tampus* were in order and the storage bins filled. Dried corn, potatoes, sun-dried llama meat, and dehydrated potatoes keep indefinitely. In time of war, when fifty thousand or more warriors might move along the road at one time, advance notice was given and abundant food stores were placed at the military's disposal—a far better commissary than that which faced the revolutionary forces of Simón Bolívar when in 1824 he made his passage of the Andes to attack the forces of imperial Spain. Then six thousand live steers for nine thousand soldiers had to be sent ahead by the Spaniards; for every hundred men, one bullock per day.[69]

There were various types of these *tampus:* those called "royal," to distinguish them from those of the ordinary kind, were reserved for the Lord-Inca or his governors when they made their inspection tours of the empire. In a list of such way stations made by the half-caste Felipe Guamán Poma de Ayala, the Ayacucho-born (1534?) chronicler of things Inca, one can see how he has distinguished them: the royal *tampus* are indicated by a building, others of less consequence by a cross, while the auxiliary, those placed in the intervals of long distance, he has marked with a circle, and he calls these by the diminutive *tambillos*. We also know much about their operation because the Spanish officials in 1543, only ten years after the conquest, had a group of Spanish officers make an inspection tour over a great part of the ancient road. Out of this came a report entitled "The Ordering of the Halting Stations [*Tampus*], the Distance of One to the Other, the Methods of the Native Cargo-bearers, and the Obligations of the Respective Spanish Overloads of Said Tambos," done in Cuzco on May 31, 1543; it reads something like ancient Greece's *Manual of Road Repairs*. It was the first of its kind in the Americas.

30 Transport

WOMAN was man's oldest beast of burden.
She was the carrier, allowing the man to be free to fight. This was true in the beginnings of every old culture. The Peruvians, the Indians Inca or pre-Inca who lived within the orbit of geographical Peru, were the only primitive Americans to develop an auxiliary to women or man for transport; this was the domesticated llama.

The llama was principally employed to transport cargo, either for war or commerce; as many as twenty-five thousand might be sent on a single convoy. Averaging eighty pounds of cargo each, they could travel about twelve miles a day. Man can outlast any animal, including the horse, especially in this up-and-down world of Peru, and can carry more than a llama and go longer distances; thus transport on the roads was shared between man and llama. The llama was not a draft animal. There is no record of it having been so used, although it can be mounted and there are many pre-Inca vases showing crippled Indians riding llamas; riding, however, was not general. Since they had no draft animals they also had no wheel, and moreover no American Indian (no matter where) had even the idea of the wheel in any of its forms (the architectural arch, the potter's wheel, or the rotary quern), and for good reason: early man migrated in a series of long-drawn waves into the Americas at the Neolithic period, before the invention of the wheel. The wheel seems to have evolved and then spread from one source within the rim of the Fertile Crescent, that section of the Middle East from which so many "new" things came. The wheel was present in India as early as 3000 B.C. The caravans which arrived there found roads already built for them; Alexander the Great was amazed at brick-laid roads made for cargo and shaded by all manner of fruit-bearing trees. Yet the idea of the wheel took a thousand years to penetrate the regions beyond. Man living out the Iron Age in Britain did not use the wheel until 2000 B.C.

It is, then, quite understandable why the American cultures never had it. First, they had no draft animals, and then they had migrated into the vacuum of the New World at a time when man, in general, still relied on his own back, or better, that of his woman, for carrying. The foot was the denominator of travel.

The litter as a means of transport seems to be world-wide. Some of the oldest illustrations of Mesopotamia, for example a relief from Ur dated 2500 B.C., shows bearers carrying a litter. Models of palanquins from Crete are dated 1600 B.C., so it is not surprising to find that the Incas were carried along their royal roads in litters. The use of litters was confined, however, to the highest nobility.

"When the Incas visited the provinces of their empire . . . they traveled in great majesty," says Cieza de León, "seated in rich litters . . . enriched with gold and silver." There were curtains to be drawn during long journeys or to protect against sun or rain, ". . . round the litter marched the Lord-Inca's guard . . . in front went five thousand slingers." There were eighty litter-bearers, men drawn from the rugged Rucana peoples, clothed in special blue livery; they ran beside the litter in teams and took turns carrying. The royal road even had resting platforms where litter-bearers could pause on steep ascents.

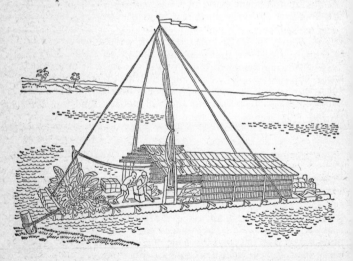

48. *The balsa raft constructed from the logs of the genus Ochroma found outside of Peru. This was the largest type of vessel known to the Peruvians. It is pre-Inca. From a drawing by Alexander von Humboldt made in 1803. Redrawn by Alberto Beltrán.*

Water transport was minor for such a thoroughly land-based people. The Incas had no concept of the sea, it was a *hatun-cocha,* a "great lake." This was one of the fundamental errors of Inca psychology in their war with the Spaniard: the Incas could not even conceive of anyone getting reinforcements from the sea. They did not fear the sea; they ignored it. It is this basic and fundamental mental block that makes historically untenable the specious arguments of those who took the *Kon-Tiki* voyage. The Incas were, in the words of Philip Ainsworth Means, "utter landlubbers."

The largest vessel known in the Americas was the Peruvian balsa raft. The logs of the balsa tree (*Ochroma*), which grows in humid Ecuador beyond the confines of the Inca realm, formed the raft. These logs, sun-dried and naturally buoyant, were lashed together with vines. The raft had a large square sail, aft of that a crude deckhouse (see von Humboldt's classical illustration of it), with palm-leaf room, and abaft of that a hearth for the preparation of food. It used the centerboard for tacking of sorts; it had no pseudo bow.[43] There is, as Means remarked, "a conspicuous lexical poverty in Quechua or any other pre-Inca coastal language on sailing, and is a reflection of the general ineptitude of the people for seamanship as a whole." The name for rafts was *huampus.*

In addition to this large raft, the coastal people (as well as the mountain people on navigable lakes) had a vessel, made of straw, called by the Spaniards (with no little humor) "little horses of the sea" in reference to the way they were used: the Indians mounted them astride. These *huampus* (also now called balsas) were made from a tubular reed which grows eight feet tall and a half inch in diameter. This swamp sedge is found at sea level as well as in the higher Andean lakes. To describe the coastal rush boat is to describe as well its highland imitation. The reed, which grows in the shore swamps, is dried and fashioned into four cigar-shaped bundles. Two of these bundles, tied with grass rope, form the prow. The other two, laid on top and off center, form its sides, and it is thus a vessel with tapering prow and square-cut stern. The sail, operating like a venetian blind, propels the boat; when there is no wind, the paddle or punt is used. Generally these boats, as shown by the old illustrations taken from Chimú or Mochica pottery, showed one, or at most three, fishermen in the boat, but on the surface of Lake Titicaca rush boats were made sufficiently large to hold forty people. These boats were also used for the floats of the Inca pontoon bridges.

Now, while rush boats are ingenious, they were by no means unique. Peoples of other cultures who lived in treeless lands, or wherever wood was not readily available, made more or less the same type of boat. The Egyptians, as one can see from the relief on the tomb of Saqqara (dated 2500 B.C.), depict workmen making a rush boat from the stems of the papyrus. Another sculpture from the tomb of Deir el-Bahri of the same epoch shows another papyrus reed boat under sail using a bipod mast (a type still used by the people of Lake Titicaca). Moreover, present-day tribes, the Dinka on the White Nile, for example, use boats made from the stems of the ambatch reeds. All these similar cultural traits, as has been consistently shown in this book, are chance parallels reached independently by people who live under similar geographical conditions; it shows how limited in imagination the human animal really is.[28]

Ne plus ultra—go no farther—was the psychological barrier that stood at the entrance of the Mediterranean into the Atlantic, and for a thousand years it kept man from venturing beyond the confines of that continent. The sea was far more of a barrier to the natives in America than to Eurasians. So fundamental was this ingrained concept that the Inca could not even conceive an invasion from the sea. Dr. George Kubler put it this way: "That which Atahualpa [the Inca captured by the Spaniards in the heart of his realm by only 130 foot soldiers and 40 mounted men] fatally misunderstood was the ability of the Spaniards to receive sea-borne reinforcements. In his experience and that of his dynastic predecessors no coastal society or state could expand beyond the wishes of a unified and powerful highland group since the ocean at their backs constituted an impassable barrier *from which no aid could come* [italics added]." [33]

It was the Inca's fatal mistake.

31 The Courier

SINCE MAN'S earliest beginnings he has attempted communications; he has shouted from hill to hill, sent smoke signals, beaten drums, tried relays of men, of horses, and carrier pigeons; he has fired cannons, but until the telegraph was invented no system of communication was as rapid as the *chasqui* courier system perfected by the Incas. It is true that other cultures had developed the relay system. That of the Persians is best known, for Herodotus himself wrote: "There is nothing in the world which travels faster than these Persian couriers, the whole idea is a Persian invention . . ."; he explains how the mounted riders were stationed along the road at intervals in posthouses and then messages passed in relays from rider to rider.

The Romans, more systematized in their communication system, relied on relays (similar to the pony-express rider of the western United States), yet even then at Rome's height (and over finely laid roads), one hundred miles a day was considered very good time. A letter traveling a thousand miles from Rome reached its designation in forty-seven days; this was considered fair time. That was the fastest communication man had ever enjoyed. With the decline of Rome such speed was never again reached until relatively recent times. That is, with the exception of the Incas.

"The Incas [again Pedro de Cieza de León is writing] invented a system of posts which was the best that could be thought of or imagined . . . and so well was this running performed that in a short time they [the Lord-Incas] knew at a distance of three hundred, five hundred or even eight hundred leagues [1 Spanish league = 2½ to 3 miles] what occurred . . . it may be certain that the news could not have been conveyed with greater speed on swift horses."

These distances seemed incredible. Yet almost all early chroniclers agree that the *chasquis* could run in relays between Quito and Cuzco, a distance of 1,250 miles, in five days—and this at an altitude ranging between 6,000 to 17,000 feet! This means that the runners had to run an average of some 250 miles a day, two and a half times faster than the Roman couriers on their metaled roads. Even fresh sea fish was said to have been relayed daily to the Lord-Inca, and the shortest distance to Cuzco from the sea was 130 miles. These statements have been alternately quoted and questioned. And with good reason, for it seemed incredible that men could run in such high altitudes without collapsing from anoxia—shortness of breath. However, the work of the von Hagen Expedition, experimenting with known and marked distances along the still extant highway, proved that the Indians could run a 6½-minute mile, and in a relay system cover this distance in the stated time.[72]

Speed was essential to the Incas. The distances were so enormous that uprisings could only be curbed by the swift marching of warriors to the center of infection. Speed, nat-

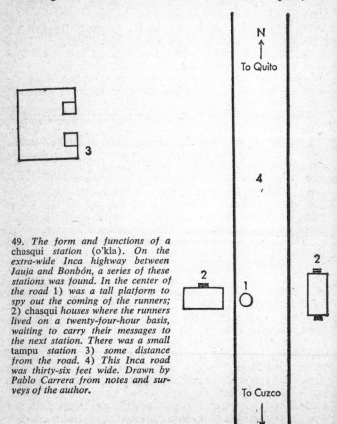

49. *The form and functions of a* chasqui *station* (o'kla). *On the extra-wide Inca highway between Jauja and Bonbón, a series of these stations was found. In the center of the road* 1) *was a tall platform to spy out the coming of the runners;* 2) chasqui *houses where the runners lived on a twenty-four-hour basis, waiting to carry their messages to the next station. There was a small* tampu *station* 3) *some distance from the road.* 4) *This Inca road was thirty-six feet wide. Drawn by Pablo Carrera from notes and surveys of the author.*

urally, is not civilization, but speed does cancel space, and the abilities of the *chasquis* to bring notice of any invasion or uprising was the prime factor in keeping the empire intact. The much quoted comment of the Confederate General Forrest, "I git thar fustest with the mostest," was precisely an Inca point of view. The time-space equation added up to the *chasqui* system; the Inca conquered space by eliminating it.

In addition to the *tampus* built along the highway there were the huts (*o'kla*) for the *chasquis* (pronounced "chaski"); rudely made and large enough to hold two men, with bed and hearth, they were placed approximately one and a half miles apart. Trained runners, with a special badge of office, waited the coming of the runners from the next station. These couriers were furnished by the village through which a particular section of the Inca road passed. They were trained from earliest youth to run at these high altitudes; games that

50. *The* chasqui, *drawn from life. This is a post-conquest drawing, He blows a conch shell to announce his arrival. In his hand he carries a mace and a slingshot for defense. Redrawn from Felipe Guamán Poma de Ayala.*

involved racing and running were part of their pageantry.
"The young sons of the nobility," said an observant Jesuit of
the sixteenth century, "used to race one another up
Huanacauri hill and to practice running; this has been and
still is [he was writing in 1570] a widely used custom
among the Indians." With his abnormally developed lungs,
the result of living in the high altitudes, the *chasqui* fitted
all the requirements of a true athlete and could run at full
speed at heights where other unacclimatized runners could
not.

It is essential to know that these courier stations were
erected within one or one and a half miles of each other, and
that the *chasqui* ran only between these points. "In each
house," said Cieza, who actually saw hundreds of such places,
"there were two Indians stationed [on a twenty-four-hour
service] with provisions. The *chasqui* then ran with
great speed without stopping, *each one for his half league*
[italics added] or mile and a half." Tests made by the von
Hagen Expedition, with natives running between those courier stations still standing, determined that they ran on average a 6½-minute mile (present record for the mile at writing is 3:54.5). It has been proven fully that the *chasquis* could
run some 250 miles a day using these relays. They could and
did cover the distance of 1,250 miles, that is from Quito to
Cuzco, in five days. The system of *chasqui* runners was so ef-
ficient that the Spanish colonial governments retained it
until 1800. There are many Spanish records in the National
Archives of Peru which prove this in detail.

The *chasquis* worked on fifteen-day shifts. Their duty was
to watch the road for the arrival of runners coming from
either direction. When the runner arrived he gave a verbal
message, along with the knot-string recordkeeper, and then
with this in hand the next courier made the run to the next
station at top speed. He was punished with death if he did
not transmit the message or divulged it to any other than the
next *chasqui*.

"With such secrecy did the runners keep their messages,"
writes Cieza, who no doubt witnessed many times the attempt
to force out of them the contents of their messages, "that
neither entreaty nor menace could extort it from them."

32 The Knot-String Record
—Inca Literature

THE *quipu* (pronounced "kee-poo"), which means simply "knot," and which the couriers passed from hand to hand, was as close to writing as man got in South America; still no matter how much writers have strained their imagination, the *quipu is not writing,* and, moreover, the device is not even an Inca invention. It is simply a mnemonic device to aid the memory and its knotted strings are based on a decimal count. Too, all *quipus* had to be *accompanied by a verbal comment,* without which the meaning would have been unintelligible.

The *quipus* have been thoroughly studied and described.[37] The *quipu* was a simple and ingenious device; it consisted of a main cord (ranging from a foot to many feet in length) and from this cord dangled smaller colored strings which had at intervals knots (*quipus*) tied into them. It has been shown most conclusively by those who have studied them that the strings were used to record numbers in a decimal system, and that there was a symbol for zero, that is, a string with an "empty space"; this allowed them to count to over ten thousand. Knots were tied into the string to represent numbers; if a governor was visiting a newly conquered tribe and the Inca wanted to know how many able-bodied Indians there were, these were counted and the number tied into the *quipu.* It may be that there was a certain symbol or heraldic device for "men," but if there was one it is not known. There was attached to the governor an official knot-string-record interpreter known as a *quipu-camayoc,* whose duty it was to tie in the records. He then had to remember which *quipu* recorded what; numbers of men, women, llamas, etc., in the newly conquered lands. When a governor had an audience with the Inca he could, with this knot-string record plus the "rememberer," recite the facts as gathered. It was a surprisingly efficacious method of counting and one that their Spanish conquerors much admired.[45]

The different colors of the wool threads apparently had meaning; the mode of intertwining the knot or twisting the thread or the distance of the knots from each other gave nuance. With these *quipus* the Inca had the numbers of tribes, llamas, women, old people.⁴ Beyond mere numbers the colors, the smaller threads, the green, blue, white, black and red colors, could, it is believed, express meanings and even, it is asserted, abstract ideas. When Pedro de Cieza de León in 1549 talked to some of the old "rememberers" they explained that these "knots counted from one to ten and ten to a hundred, and from a hundred to a thousand. Each ruler of a province was provided with accountants, and by these knots they kept account of what tribute was to be paid . . . and with such accuracy that not so much as a pair of sandals would be missing.

"I was incredulous respecting this system of counting and although I heard it described, I held the greater part of the story to be fabulous. But when I was in Marca-vilca, in the province of Xauxa [i.e., central Peru near to present-day Huancayo] I asked one of them to explain the *quipu* in such a way that my curiosity would be satisfied . . . the *quipu-camayoc* proceeded to make the thing clear to me . . . he knew all that had been delivered to Francisco Pizarro, without fault or omission, since his arrival in Peru. Thus I saw all the accounts for the gold, the silver, the clothes, the corn, the llamas and other things, so that in truth I was astonished."

Like all preliterate peoples, they had good memories. While the *quipu* itself could not be read without verbal comment to make all the entanglements and knots understandable, it did (this much is certain) go beyond mere compilation of statistics; it was used as a supplement for the memory of historical events.

When a Lord-Inca died and his burial ceremonies were over, a council of *amautas* was called into session to decide "what of his memory should be forever preserved." ¹⁴ Having decided this among themselves, they composed their history and then called in the *quipu-camayocs* and gave them the official history; then those skilled in rhetoric and the use of words—and they knew how to narrate the event in regular order like ballad singers—were brought in, and *thus they were instructed* what to say concerning the deceased Inca, and if they treated of wars, they sang in proper order of the many battles he had fought.

The wholesale destruction of the "archives" of *quipus* by the crusading padres in the seventeenth century (in their zeal to stamp out idolatry, believing naively that the *quipus* "were books of the devil" ⁵⁷) and the gradual dying out of the "rememberers," the interpreters of the *quipus*, were the twin disasters to Andean history. With the destruction of one and the passing of the other there was lost that history of the whole Andean area which now can be bridged only by archaeology. The *quipus* now found in graves tell us nothing; they are only lifeless strings.

They were obviously neither alphabet nor hieroglyphs, though the amusing book written by a baroque Italian, Prince Sansevero, of Naples,[56] in the eighteenth century, in which he illustrated Peruvian *quipus* with all forms of glyphs attached to them, claimed for the *quipu* an "alphabet" and even claimed that he was able to read them. Obviously faked, as Johann Winckelmann, the famous German art historian, well knew, such an interpretation is impossible except for the lunatic fringe of archaeologic enthusiasts who read about the lost continent of Mu and its minor appendages. It is now fully established, as it has long been surmised, that *no South American people possessed writing*.

Yet history was transmitted with their aid. "Suppose," wrote Padre Calancha in 1638, "that a functionary wishes to express that before Manco Capac, the *first Inca,* there was neither king, chief, cult or religion; that in the *fourth* year of his reign this emperor subdued *ten* provinces, whose conquest cost him a certain number of men; that in one of them he took a *thousand* units of gold, and *three thousand* units of silver, and that in thanksgiving for the victory he had celebrated a festival in honor of the god, Sun." [12] All this, then, would be done on a *quipi,* tying knots in the decimal divisions, using certain colored knots symbolizing "gold," "Inca," or "Sun."

There is no lack of confirmation from contemporary sources of the ability of the professional knot-string readers to interpret them, "with as much ease," said Cieza de León, "as we in our language understood from paper and ink." An intriguing fellow, Pedro Sarmiento de Gamboa, navigator, warrior, and executioner (he exterminated the surviving members of the royal Inca line), confirmed the use of the *quipus* as histories. He was asked by his viceroy to write an official history of the Incas, which was to be an apologia for the Spanish conquest. He started in 1569 by assembling all those chieftains who knew of the past Inca history and took down what they told him. He explained in the beginning of his own history how the "barbarians of this Land" transmitted history one to another, from fathers to sons, "persisting in the repetition until it was fixed in the memory— history, exploits, antiquities, the number of tribes, towns and provinces, days, months, years, deaths, destructions, fortresses and leaders, the number of cords which they called *quipus.* . . ."

In this way and manner Inca history was conveyed. First it was selected, then memorized by means of the *quipus*, then given to the troubadours to chant, as Pedro de Cieza de León noted: ". . . they used a kind of folk-poems and romances by means of which they would retain a memory of events and without forgetting them."

This was the manner in which the Incas made a "selective manipulation of history," as discussed earlier in this book. They blotted out whole generations of racial memory of the tribes which had preceded them so that they could pose as *the* culture bearers. This system began with the Lord-Inca called Pachacuti ("crowned" Inca in 1438). After he had rebuilt Cuzco he called together the professional *quipu-camayocs*. He had them tell him their histories. Then he had these painted on the wall in chronological order, ". . . and into this room no one could enter except the Lord-Inca." That which was distasteful to the Inca was eliminated from official memory—the *quipu* did not speak of it, the romancers did not sing of it; in this way much of pre-Inca history was eliminated. Such a performance is not wholly incredible. The Soviet Encyclopedia today can eliminate well-known personalities by sending to its subscribers new pages to replace its censored pages. People disappear from life and become, in the Orwellian phrase, "unpersons." During World War II, 100,000 Caucasians of the Kabard and Balkar mountain-dwelling tribesmen were deported as alleged "collaborators." Their names were dropped, their literature suppressed, their whereabouts kept secret; only recently have they emerged.

The lack of writing in any form among the South Americans is at once a puzzle and a problem; it renders the chronology of the cultures exceedingly difficult and makes us fall back on an oral history and archaeology. It is a cultural hiatus, almost without parallel. The Aztecs had pictographic writing and were arriving at the stage of syllabic phonetics when the Spaniards arrived. The Maya glyphic writing, far earlier than the Aztec, and far more advanced, was sufficiently perfected as to work out a very involved calendar; they have left behind a corpus of glyphic inscriptions which will occupy Maya scholars for many years to come. Even the North American Plains Indians had a form of rebus writing which by puns, positions, color, and crude drawings conveyed ideas. There was no such thing in South America; and unbelievably no writing among the Incas, who needed it most of all. There has been an attempt by Señor Rafael Larco of Trujillo, Peru, to interpret the "beans" painted on Mochica pottery as a glyphic language. This study, more extensive than

51. *A woman of the Quechua tribe in her dress of the Inca period. She beats a drum. Redrawn from Felipe Guamán Poma de Ayala.*

any published, has been given short shrift by the professionals. It needs to be carried further; beyond this we are in the same position as the first Spaniards who said *the Incas had no form of writing.*

One scholar dismisses the need for writing, saying, "The fact is that the Andean peoples possessed substitutes for writing which were so satisfactory that they probably never felt the need for anything more elaborate." [53] Such a conclusion is praise of intellectual castration; it belies the whole of cultural history. For of all discoveries and inventions, writing gave us the continuity of what we are pleased to call civilization; even the cave man used pictographs, the first writing forms, and as man became Man and formed himself into societies with cities, tribute, and trade, writing became part of life. The need forced the invention; writing was a *must* if only for economic reasons.

The Sumerians, who lived in that Fertile Crescent of the Middle East, seemed to have invented it circa 4000 B.C., and it then spread. The Phoenicians developed the alphabet sometime before 1000 B.C., and it became a cultural lever. "Give me but a place to stand and I can move the world," said Archimedes. Writing did just that. Our knowledge of the Romans would be very vague if they, like the Incas, had had no form of writing. Dated Roman coins found in India suggest their presence there; outside the purlieus of the Roman frontier, in northern Germany or Denmark, the presence of dated coins tells the approximate date of Roman conquests; their literature supplies the details. Literature *fixed* historical traditions; it strengthened social cohesion. Would it not be impossible to know the Greeks without their literature, or the Romans without their interminable reports, or the Egyptians without their long and involved personal histories as told in the hieratic glyphs?

Still if the Incas had no writing, they had a form of literature, which has come down to us by oral tradition. Yet it soon becomes obvious that since there was no writing, there is no "pure" literature; the literature has undergone the alchemy of change, in translation, in meter, even in idea and symbol. It is, however, quite obvious that a people who were so saturated with symbol and pageantry would have lyrical verse, and although unrhymed it at least was cadenced, for it is in rhythm that one remembers best. Those fragments of Inca "literature" that have come down to us were gathered by some of the earlier writers, notably Inca-Spaniard Garcilaso de la Vega (who affected the verse and ideas of seventeenth-century Spain) as well as others. These cadences were remembered from the professional bards (*haravecs*), who chanted them at festivals or before the court. This particular verse, said Garcilaso, surnamed "the Inca," was preserved by the *quipu*. (He does not say how, and this is not surprising in view of the limitations.)

> *Beautiful Princess,*
> *thy dear brother*
> *thy cup*
> *is now breaking.*
> *So for this there is thunder,*
> *lightning, lightning*
> *thunderbolts falling,*
> *But Princess,*
> *thy water*

> *dropping, rains*
> *where sometimes also*
> *there will be hail,*
> *there will be snow.*
> *The maker of the earth,*
> *Pachacamac*
> *Viracocha,*
> *for this duty*
> *has placed thee,*
> *has created thee.*

The ideas, the cadence, the repetition, the imagery, is decidedly Inca. And from Felipe Guamán Poma de Ayala, an Inca-Spaniard of the same epoch as Garcilaso, comes this cadenced prose. He did not see the courts of Spain, and was not seduced by the gilded ennui of Spanish poets: what he gives here would seem reasonably pure, reasonably Inca. As an Indian woman plants her corn she chants:

> *Pity my tears,*
> *Pity my anguish.*
> *The most distressed*
> *Of your children,*
> *The most distressed*
> *Implores you with tears,*
> *Grant the miracle*
> *Of water, your own,*
> *Grant the gift of rain*
> *To this unfortunate*
> *Person,*
> *To this creature*
> *You have created.*

Another from the same source—a touching love song:

> *To this my song,*
> *You shall sleep,*
> *In the dead of night*
> *I shall come.*

There are others, which the late Philip Ainsworth Means selected as undoubtedly coming from the official festivals. This has all the majesty of ritual:

> *Viracocha, Lord of the Universe.*
> *Whether male or female*
> *Anyway, commander of warmth and generation.*

> *Being one who*
> *Even with his spittle can work magic.*
> *Where are you?"*
> *Would that you would not hide from this your son.*
> *He may be above,*
> *He may be below,*
> *Or alight in the sky,*
> *Where is his council seat,*
> *Hear me!*

There were many others, and many of them have been collected and published as "Quechua poetry," [35] but all are suspect for the very reason that without written literature no one is in a position to challenge the translator as to the source. So when a verse begins as though an Indian is weeping for his dead wife:

> *What cruel land has buried*
> *Her who was my only joy?*

and continues in such lyrical sentiments as:

> *I scrabble the tomb where she sleeps*
> *While my tears flow like rain, endlessly,*
> *Thus should the earth be softened,*

you may be instantly aware that this is not Quechua poetry; it is modern contrivance.

The best known Inca dramatic piece—the drama of *Ollantay*—was long thought to have been "pure Inca" and was acted in some of the semicircular arenas thought to have been Inca theaters.* The place itself is historic; Ollantaytambo (see Figure 35) lies twenty-four miles from Cuzco in the valley of Yucay on the upper Urubamba River. Early in the fifteenth century Ollantaytambo was ruled by semi-independent chieftains. They disputed with the Inca, who sacked and destroyed the original site and rebuilt the formidable place—still to be seen. The Incas were still building it when the Spaniards arrived in 1536 and continued to build it even

---

* A number of older writers believed that *Ollantay* was a pre-conquest composition, but this view is now thoroughly discredited. The English translation of 1871 was made by Sir Clements Markham; it was reissued as an appendix to his work *The Incas of Peru* in 1910. This play is perhaps the best-known example of Inca literature; it has been translated into Spanish (1868), English (1871), German (1875), French (1878), and Czech (1917–18). In 1941 the Argentine writer Ricardo Rojas published a modified version of it which was a notable stage success in Buenos Aires.

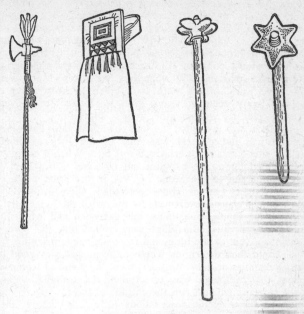

52. *Ceremonial Mace*
Shield
Stone-headed Mace
War Ax

Made from plaited llama wool, measuring from fourteen to twenty-eight inches when doubled, it was fearfully and simply made; it had a sort of egg-size cradle for the stone. The sling was whirled about the head, an end released, and the stone shot forward to its mark with great accuracy; it could dent a steel helmet at fifteen yards, stunning the man in it (as the Spaniards could testify); without the protection of a helmet, the injury inflicted by the sling-tossed stone was fatal. The closing-in weapon was the mace, a three-foot-long wooden shaft, topped with a heavy bronze or stone star-shaped piece at its "business end." Its effectiveness is borne out by the number of crushed skulls found which had been operated on to relieve the pressure on the brain from such blows. In addition, the Incas used a sort of double-edged sword made from *chonta* wood and used like the two-handed broadsword of the sixteenth century. These were their weapons.

Since man *is* war, it is useless to discuss causes; they arose among the Incas as they do among us: survival, aggrandizement, pressure, caprice, necessary and unnecessary reasons, but since the Incas were dedicated to bring the religion of the Sun as well as "Inca civilization" to all people (with that fearful dedication so well known to militant Christianity), war was almost constant. Either the Incas were conquering new peoples, or defending what they had taken. Many were preventive wars; others were undertaken to keep the professional army occupied, says John H. Rowe, "to prevent generals plotting against the Inca's succession."

The Inca was expected to lead his men into battle, or when it was not general war, one of the Inca's intimate circle, a blood relative, performed this task. When a conquest was decided upon, the captains, all *Orejones* ("Big Ears"), were summoned to the Stone of War in the great plaza of Cuzco. Diviners (*kalpa-rikoqs*) were then called forth—those who were specialists in divining by means of the lungs of the sacred black llama. The llama was cut open and while the llama was still alive the lungs were pulled out; the diviner blew into a vein of the lung, and from the vague markings on it he would then determine whether the augury was good or bad. One smiles at this? Consider, then, the civilized Romans: before any campaign was undertaken the captains looked to the sacred chickens, and the entrails of the fowl were consulted. If these occult observations forbade a victory, they were not supposed to go into battle. One consul in the First Punic War was so angry at having his carefully laid plans frustrated by a contrary opinion that he killed the sacred chickens. One sees from this how close the Incas were to the heart of the matter.

If war then was decided upon, the word went out. Warriors were summoned and, on arrival, placed in companies corresponding to their *ayllus*. Each wore the totemic device of his clan. All warriors were, of course, classified by the decimal system. It is related how the Lord-Inca Huayna Capac (died 1527) made war. He was "a man of few words but many deeds, a severe judge who punished without mercy. He wished to be so feared that his Indians would dream of him at night." He set out for the conquest of Quito with 300,000 soldiers; roads were made ready, the enemy ahead was scouted, the *tampus* along the roads filled with food, the llamas assembled to carry, supplemented by thousands of human carriers. The army on the march was severely disciplined. No warrior was allowed off the road to steal or bother the civilians; penalty, death.

Now the reason for the wide, well-kept roads is fully apparent—conquest.

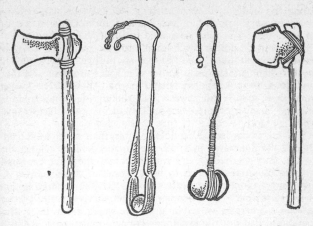

53. *War Ax*
    Sling
    Mace
    War Ax

When the enemy was sighted, the Incas's troops did what all their enemies did, they blew their horns, shouted insults, trying to overwhelm them in a chaos of sound; for this reason their Spanish enemy characterized them all as "brown and noisy." But with the Incas the object of the battle was to win it; war for them was not, as it had been with pre-Incans, ritualistic promenades, elaborate panoplies to overawe an enemy; they had but a single object—victory. They had neither superior weapons nor superior tactics, but they had discipline, and a good system of supply and roads; roads decided it. The object of these roads, then, was not economic but military, to get their warriors there and in mass.

Battle began with the slingers tossing their hail of stones, while those armed with the *macanas* advanced. Spears were thrown at short distances; then the warriors closed in with the mace. Once battle was joined, it was a formless melee. They used ambush and the burning of grass to force the enemy into positions to be attacked by mass. If they attacked hilltop fortresses, they advanced under a canopy of hides shaped into shields to protect them from the slingshot missiles. If the enemy took refuge in a building, firehot stones were hurled to burn the grass thatch and force them out into the open. The formlessness of Inca battle, once it was joined, was a tactical error that the Spaniards exploited to the full, and that is why a Spanish *capitán* could boast: "I took no more notice of a hundred armed Indians than I would have of a handful of flies." [48]

There was another traditional weakness in Inca warfare which they practiced, like all Andean people. They launched most of their attacks on the advent of the full moon and they kept to a twenty-day rhythm of battle. They rarely fought in mass at night. All these ritual tactics, when understood by their Spanish enemy, were used with marked effect against them.

Yet the Incas learned quickly. After their swift initial defeat by the Spaniards in 1532, they made defense against the horses, they learned to fire the arquebus, they put captured Spanish munitions makers to work; some of them learned to ride horses. In the neo-Inca state (1537-72), operating out of the sanctuary of Vilcapampa, the surviving Lord-Incas and their warriors waged a guerrilla warfare for thirty-five years, and had not the last Inca, Tupac Amaru, been seduced by "honied words" they might have prevailed.

Once the Incas decided on the conquest of a given territory, no force in the Andes could stem the tide of their wave of the future; the Incas never lost a battle of importance after 1437, and the violence, from all surviving accounts, was sufficiently awesome. There was a wholesale slaughter of the defeated in the field and a ceremonial slaughter later. A warrior was decorated for killing (one man killed, one of the warrior's arms was painted black; two killed, his chest was painted; three killed, a black mark was painted across the face between both ears, etc.). The Incas were not as blood-thirsty as were the Aztecs, but captives were taken, led in triumph through Cuzco, and forced to lie prone in front of the Sun Temple as the Inca trod upon their necks, symbolizing the victory. Heads were taken from the more ferocious of the enemy and made into drinking cups (as with the Vikings). If the enemy was especially hated, they flayed the captives alive, then stuffed their skins in a ridiculous mimicry of life, making the stomachs into drums which they beat when warming themselves up for battle. A sort of museum of these stuffed skins of the Chanca tribe—hereditary enemies of the Inca who had the temerity to attack sacred Cuzco in 1437—was seen by the Spaniards when they entered Peru. Yet the Inca policy generally was: conquer by arms, reconcile by kindness.

The Organization and
34 Assimilation of Conquered Lands

T HE INCAS organized their conquests as they organized every-thing else in their world. The methods of other South American tribes before their coming had been to raid, loot, take slaves, levy tribute, and return to their tribal lands; only the religio-military conquest of Tiahuanaco (circa A.D. 1000 –1300) had attempted to assimilate all Peru, but this failed and they left behind (see page 29) only vague memories of their cult of the Weeping God.

The Incas were masters of organization. They turned con-quest into empire. They began their political life, circa A.D. 1100, in the limited orbit of the Cuzco Valley. At this time the whole of the Andean and coastal areas of the land which one day was to be Inca were broken into an almost unbelievable number of small and great tribes of different tongues and customs. By 1500, the Incas had absorbed every one of these tribes—conservatively estimated at over five hundred—into their empire which stretched all the way from Argentina to Colombia, from the shores of the Pacific into the Upper Amazon. It was one of the great empires of all time, totaling 350,000 square miles, equivalent to the land mass compre-hended in the Atlantic seaboard states of North America. The conquests were gradual: first the immediate territory was taken around Cuzco, then beyond to the south, then to the west, then to the north; only when they were fully tested did the Inca's armies try to come to grips with the people of the jungle to the east.

No sooner had the new territory fallen into their con-quering maw than a census of all the people was taken by means of the *quipus*. If the conquered were still belligerent, they were liquidated; if they were a valiant foe they were treated with considerable kindness. Local customs and dress and language were respected; the local language was allowed, but officials had to learn Quechua.

The Sun replaced all other religions, yet if their local

gods were efficacious they were adopted into the Inca pantheon. Local chieftains either were put to death, or sent to Cuzco as hostages and trained to the "new order," then sent back and allowed to keep their titles. A relief model, clay or stone, was made of the territory and taken to Cuzco along with a census of people, animals, agriculture. If the principle of the *ayllu*, the earth cell, was not already in operation, it was established on Inca lines. The roads which had been built up to the border of the territory to be seized were now extended through the conquered lands, which were integrated into the empire. Professional architects were sent out from Cuzco and directed the building of a new urban center, and especially the Temple of the Sun. If the whole population was irreconcilable, then they were moved out bodily— as the Soviets do today—and the vacuum filled by *mitimaes*, Quechua-speaking peoples loyal to the Inca. They were moved into the conquered lands, often many hundreds of miles from their original homes; population transference was an important part of Inca policy. The *mitimaes* were of three orders: military, political, and economic. Quechua-speaking soldiers were quartered in frontier stations, some as far away as the Paraguayan *chaco*, or at the bridgeheads in the Amazon, to prevent incursions of wild tribes. Political *mitimaes* were settled, for example, in the Chachapoyas region won to the empire circa A.D. 1480. Economic *mitimaes* were settled in humid areas of the Montaña east of Cuzco to raise the coca leaf, to name one instance. There were innumerable other population transfers into regions which were uninhabited. Where there was a bridge to be guarded as at Uranmarca, to give but one example, they erected a *marca* above it with the sole object of keeping in repair the second largest suspension bridge in all Peru, that which crossed the Vilcas (now Pampas) River, which lay beyond the great Inca center of Vilcas-huamán.

By peopling thinly populated regions, by placing *mitimaes* in regions devoid of population so that the roads would be kept open, the bridges repaired, etc., the Incas welded the land into empire.

"One of the things for which one feels envious of these Lords-Incas," wrote that wonderful observer Pedro de Cieza de León, "is their knowledge of the way to conquer . . . and to bring them by good management into empire. I often remember when in some wild and barren province outside of these kingdoms [of the Incas] hearing Spaniards themselves say, 'I am certain that if the Incas had been here the state of things would be different' . . .

"In all things the *system* [i.e., replacing buildings, damaged by war, bringing in llamas where needed, sending in official builders, instructing the newly conquered how to cultivate their fields better] was so well regulated that when one of the Incas entered into a new province . . . in a very short time it looked like another place . . . In other words, those who conquered by force of arms were given an order that as little harm should be done to property and houses of the vanquished as was possible; for the Lord-Inca said:

" 'These will soon be our people as much as others.' "

So then these *mitimaes* were civilizers as the Roman soldiers were civilizers; each group was a representative of order—soldier and agriculturist, road builder and bringer of civilization.

So complete was this integration of the Andes and the coast of that part which lay in the Inca realm, that the Inca style was etched indelibly in the land. "One short century of Inca rule [1400–1500]," writes Dr. John Rowe,[53] "completely altered the course of Andean cultural history." To this day Inca provincial boundaries and names are widely used and the Inca language flourishes (spoken by upwards of five million people), while even the memory of the older states and languages has vanished. And so the whole Andean area is colored indelibly with the Inca dye.

And to this day, in every part of the territory ruled by the Incas, one is hourly conscious of the ghost of the Incas' supremacy manifesting itself in a score of ways: through speech, customs, and material culture.

Thus stood the realm of the Incas on that fatal day of 1527, when a small Spanish caravel, no more than ten tons burthen, sailed into Tumbes.

35 Decline

WHY AND HOW did such a benevolent despotism fall so quickly? How was it possible for only 130 foot soldiers and 40 cavalry with but one small falconet-cannon able to penetrate the Andes, seek out the Lord-Inca surrounded by fifty thousand warriors, and then in one skirmish—which lasted precisely 33 minutes—psychologically reduce by that bold action this great realm of the Incas? The question has been asked over and over again through these centuries, and no one has yet come up with a satisfactory answer, just as there have been thousands of books to attempt to explain the decline and fall of Rome. There are, however, some historical details which might help explain this decline and fall of the Inca Empire.

By 1493, when Huayna Capac was "crowned" Lord-Inca, the Inca Empire had almost reached its greatest heights. After a series of setbacks in his attempt to bring some of the jungle Indians in northern Ecuador and Colombia under control, he finally set the limits to the most northern realm at the Ancasmayo River (1° N. lat.) in the mountains, and Tumbes (3° S. lat.) on the coast. Like the Roman Emperor Hadrian, this last great Inca attempted to set limits to his realm.

There is a natural limit to conquest, and that is the power of assimilation. Time gnawed at the bones of the old Inca, who had to consider who among all his hundreds of male heirs would be named Inca. The first years of this "setting bounds to the fields" were ones of inward peace within the Inca realm, but in the later years of the reign of Huayna Capac there was disquieting news from without. The later years were full of gloom and evil portent.* In defeating a tribe in the Chaco region there had been reported the presence of a strange man, white and bearded, among the enemy. There were further reports, vague and contradictory yet persistent, of other white men sailing in large ships down the Pacific coast.

The Peruvians had little concept of humanity beyond their

---

* For a detailed discussion of this see Philip Ainsworth Means, *Ancient Civilizations of the Andes.*

own sphere, nor of geography beyond the immediate; they had no direct contact with either the Mayas or the Aztecs. They were completely unaware of their existence. The Aztecs were conquered in 1521 and the Mayas set upon in 1527; this must have produced shock waves (since the Mayas traded as far south as Panama) which were felt in Peru even though uncomprehended. All contact with these other civilizations was only by a geographical filtration. The Incas had emeralds, for instance, which occur in the Americas only in the mines in Colombia, but they had them not by direct contact; they filtered down to them from tribe to tribe.

The people of Panama had known white man since the time that Columbus in 1502 had set up a colony near to the isthmus. Nuñez de Balboa had wandered to the Pacific as early as 1513, yet none of this information came down in tangible pattern to the Incas. For the Indians of Panama, too, had only the vaguest idea of this great realm to the south; it came to their common ken by means of a multiple cascade of interpretations, so that all an Indian chieftain could do when pressed by the conquest-hungry Spaniards for news of other lands, was to model in clay for Capitán Pascal de Andogoya in 1522 on some muddied shore of Darien, an animal, which the Indian meant to be a llama (but which the Spaniards mistook for a sheep), saying that the people who had such "sheep" were those of the Kingdom of Gold.

It is important that this lack of direct contact between the great American civilizations be stressed; they were, so far as we know now, in complete unawareness of each other's existence. If there had been such contact, then that terrible catastrophe of the Conquest of Mexico in 1521 would have been transmitted to the Incas, and they would have put themselves into a state of defense for a doom which could have been deduced. Yet they must have received vague rumors, through trade that passed from hand to hand coming down from Mexico to Panama, Colombia to Peru, of something that was occurring, and vague foreboding settled over the land. A pestilence at this time came to Peru, and although it cannot be positively identified, it was new in their experience and could have been one of the diseases, perhaps smallpox, brought by the Spaniard.

Then, toward the end of Huayna Capac's reign, an Inca outpost in the Chaco was attacked by Chiriguano Indians led by a white man. That man we now know was a Spaniard named Alego García, who, captured by Indians in Brazil, had become their captain. The time was 1525.

Two years later, Francisco Pizarro arrived at Tumbes with his famous "thirteen men of Gallo"; they embraced the natives, traded gewgaws, shot off guns, skirted the Peruvian coast, and then took Indians aboard to train them as interpreters for their contemplated return. Pizarro left behind for future use two Spaniards, one named Alonso de Molina, and a Negro, Gines. All these strange marvels were transmitted to the Inca, who in 1527 lay on his death bed.

Huayna Capac then died without naming his successor. As will be recalled, when discussing the Inca as state (see page 116, there was no fixed rule of descent; the Inca chose with advice from his council the most competent of his sons born of his principal queen, the *coya*. Now that son whom most considered would be made Inca was Huáscar, who resided in Cuzco, and in default of a clear line of descent he was proclaimed Inca, but the deceased Inca had among his numerous subsidiary offspring one named Atahualpa, who was born in the region which is now Ecuador and who traveled much with Huayna Capac in his later years, and was personally known and much liked by the principal generals of the army.

The result of this dispute for Inca-ship was a devastating civil war between the two brothers which lasted five years, corresponding precisely with the intervening years when Francisco Pizarro was in Spain organizing for his conquest of the Kingdom of Gold.

In the final battle Huáscar was captured, his generals killed, thousands of Indians slaughtered, and Atahualpa's generals were sent to Cuzco to put to death as many of Huáscar's family as they could apprehend, and also to prepare the capital for Atahualpa's entry into Cuzco to be proclaimed Inca.

At this precise moment Francisco Pizarro arrived with his small army at Tumbes; the date: May 13, 1532.

Atahualpa (who was to be proclaimed Inca) was at this time taking the hot sulphur baths at Cajamarca, a place then of no great importance in the Inca realm. He was awaiting the reports from his *chasquis* from Cuzco about the preparations for his triumphant entry. He was surrounded by his battle-tried warriors, men who had fought this terrible fratricidal war for five years. He was the master now of everything, everyone in the domain; he could lop off the head of his most famous general merely by raising his hand; he could do it even by long distance via a messenger. It was then at this moment that he received messages from the coast of the arrival of the Spaniards.

His intelligence was exact; the *quipus* counted out the number of men and animals (so strange that no one could give them a name except that they thought man and beast were one). It was the *interpretation* of this intelligence that was faulty: The animals had feet of silver (the horseshoes gave that effect), they were impotent at night; if the rider fell off the animal that ended both. As for the guns which spouted fire, they were only thunderbolts and could only be fired twice. One of the coastal chieftains, so the report said, poured a libation of corn *chicha* into a barrel of one of the guns so as to solace the thunder god. Moreover, the steel swords of these bearded men were as ineffectual as women's weaving battens. From all this it shows that the Inca had absolutely no advance notice of the white man. It is true that at first Atahualpa thought that they were returning gods, for it was legend that the Inca's creator-god, Tici Viracocha, who had helped bring civilization to them, had been dissatisfied with his handiwork and sailed away and would someday return (this is a persistent legend throughout the Americas about ships returning over the ocean sea, and must somewhere have substance).

For when a chieftain himself puffed up the Andes to report: "People have arrived by a big ship from out of the *hatun-cocha* [sea], with different clothing, beards and animals like llamas, only larger," Atahualpa thought that the gods themselves were coming to conduct him to Cuzco to his rightful heritage as Inca. Still he was no fool. After he had reports on the Spaniards' progress and heard how they raped his Virgins of the Sun at the village of Caxas, he knew by then that he dealt with no gods.

His strategy, supposedly, *since he believed as all other Indians did that no one could get reinforcements from the sea,* was to offer no resistance, draw them in, set them down neatly in one of the towns, perhaps at Cajamarca itself, give the signal, and that would be finis to this little episode which delayed his trip to Cuzco. For what had Atahualpa to fear? He was god. He was surrounded by thousands of warriors, and against so small a number . . . So then he accepted—we believe naively, but to him it was doubtless a whim of those about to die—an invitation from the Spaniards to visit their chieftain Francisco Pizarro in the plaza at Cajamarca. His warriors were to come unarmed "so as not to give offense."

It was at vespers during the early evening of November 16, 1532,[17] when the Inca, carried in his litter and surrounded by an unarmed bodyguard, moved into the plaza of Cajamarca. There was, if one will recall reading Prescott's *Conquest of Peru,* an unintelligible parley between Christian priest and Inca god, then that one cannon belched out its

thunder into the ranks of brown bodies, and with the cry of
"Santiago!" and "At them!" the Spaniards ambushed the
hapless Inca.

The rest is history.

Bibliography

1. Acosta, José de, *The Naturall and Morall Historie of the East and West Indies.* London, 1604.
   A very learned and balanced Jesuit, whose intellectual love of God did not blind him to the good qualities of the Indian; this book is notable since it deals with Acosta's travels in Mexico and Peru as early as 1565. He compares the cultures, he is colorful and accurate. When obtained (which will be difficult) the work should be read.

2. Adam, Leonhard, *Primitive Art,* 3rd rev. ed. Harmondsworth, England, 1954.

3. Allier, Raoul, *The Mind of the Savage,* trans. by Fred Rothwell. New York, 1929.

4. Altieri, Radamés A., "Sobre II Antiguos Kipu Peruanos," *Revista del Instituto de Antropológia de la Universidad Nacional de Tucumán,* vol. II (1941), 177-211.

5. Anonymous Conqueror, *Anonymous La Conquista del Peru,* Seville, April, 1534.
   (See a critical reprint, edited by Dr. A. Pogo, in Proc. Am. Acad. of Arts and Scs., vol. 64, No. 8, July, 1930.)

6. Barrow, R. H., *The Romans.* Harmondsworth, England, 1949.

7. Baudin, Louis, *L'Empire Socialiste des Inka.* Paris, 1928.

8. Bennett, Wendell, *Ancient Arts of the Andes.* New York, 1954.

9. ———, and Bird, Junius B., *Andean Culture History.* American Museum of Natural History, Handbook Series, no. 15. New York, 1949.

10. Bingham, Hiram, *Lost City of the Incas: the Story of Machu Picchu and its Builders.* New York, 1948.

11. Borah, Woodrow, *Early Colonial Trade and Navigation Between Mexico and Peru.* Berkeley, Calif., 1954.

12. Calancha, Antonio de la, *Cronica moralizada del orden de San Augustin en el Perú . . .* Barcelona, 1638.

13. Childe, V. Gordon, "Early Forms of Society," in Singer, et al. (eds.), *A History of Technology,* vol. 1.

14. Cieza de León, Pedro de, *The Travels of Pedro de Cieza de León,* trans. and ed. by Clements R. Markham. London, 1864.
    But see a new edition of these famous chronicles, translated by Harriet de Onis, edited by Victor Wolfgang von Hagen, published by the University of Oklahoma Press, Norman, 1959.

15. Cobo, Bernabé, *Historia del Nuevo Mundo,* 4 vols. Seville, 1890-93.

16. Doughty, Charles, *Travels in Arabia Deserta.* New York, 1923.

17. Estete, Miguel de, *Noticias del Peru,* Col. Libr. Documentos, Ref. de Historia del Peru, vol. 8, Lima, Peru, 1924.

18. Fejos, Pál, *Archeological Explorations in the Cordillera Vilcabamba, Southeastern Peru.* New York, 1944.

19. Forbes, R. J., "Chemical, Culinary and Cosmetic Arts," in Singer, et al. (eds.), *A History of Technology,* vol. 1.

20. Ford James A., "The History of a Peruvian Valley," *Scientific American,* vol. 191, no. 12 (August, 1954), 28-34.

21. Garcilaso de la Vega, *Primera Parte de los Commentarios reales . . . ,* Lisboa, 1609.
    (There is an English edition of Garcilaso translated by Sir Clements Markham and published by the Haykluyt Society, London, 1869.)

22. Gazin, C. Lewis, *Review of the Upper Eocene Artiodactyla of North America.* Smithsonian Miscellaneous Collection, vol. 128, no. 8. Washington, D. C., 1955.

23. Graña, Francisco, Rocca, Esteban R., and Graña R., Luis, *Las Trepanaciones Craneanas en el Perú en la Epoca pre-Hispanica.* Lima, 1954.

24. Gutuérrez Noriega, Carlos, and von Hagen, V. W., "The Strange Case of the Coca Leaf," *Scientific Monthly,* vol. 70, no. 2 (February, 1950), 81-9.

25. Harcourt, Raoul and Marie d', *La Musique des Incas et ses Survivances.* Paris, 1925.

26. Harth-terré, Emilio, Drawings in Means, *Ancient Civilization of the Andes,* N. Y., 1931.

27. Heyerdahl, Thor, *Kon-Tiki: Across the Pacific by Raft,* trans. by F. H. Lyon. Chicago, 1951.

28. Hornell, J., "South American Balsas; The Problem of Their Origin," *The Mariners' Mirror,* vol. XVII, 347-55.

29. Humboldt, Alexander von, *Vues des Cordillères et Monuments des Peuples Indigènes de l'Amérique,* Paris, 1810.
    Humboldt was the great figure of the opening of the nineteenth

century. After explorations in South America, Cuba, and Mexico, he compiled a vast amount of data extraordinary in both its range and its accuracy. This work is a landmark in American archaeology but now little used since the volume is in folio and is expensive. Yet it deserves to be reconsidered. His attitude toward archaeological remains as fragments of history laid the solid base of American scholarship. He was the first to stress the oneness of indigenous culture.

30. Huxley, Julian, *From an Antique Land.* London and New York, 1954.

31. Jenison, Madge, *Roads.* New York, 1948.

32. Jimenez, Arturo, *Instrumentos Musicales del Perú.* Lima, 1951.

33. Kubler, George, "The Quechua in the Colonial World," in Steward (ed.), *Handbook of South American Indians,* vol. 2.

34. Larco Hoyle, Rafael, "La Escritura Peruana Sobre Pallares," *Revista Geográfica Americana,* Año 11, vol. 20, nos. 122-3 (1943), 93-103.

35. Lata, Jesús, *La Poesía Quechua.* La Paz, 1949.

36. Lévy-Bruhl, Lucien, *Primitives and the Supernatural,* trans. by Lilian A. Clare. New York, 1935.

37. Locke, L. Leland, *The Ancient Quipu or Peruvian Knot Record.* New York, 1923.

38. Lothrop, Samuel K., *Inca Treasure as Depicted by Spanish Historians.* Los Angeles, 1938.

39. Mangelsdorf, Paul, and Reeves, Robert G., *The Origin of Indian Corn and Its Relatives.* Texas Agricultural Experiment Station, Bulletin 574. College Station, Texas, 1939.

40. Markham, Sir Clements R., *Cuzco: A Journey to the Ancient Capital of Peru; and Lima: A visit to the Capital and Province of Modern Peru.* London, 1856.

41. Means, Philip Ainsworth, *Ancient Civilizations of the Andes.* New York, 1931.

42. ———, *Fall of the Inca Empire and the Spanish Rule in Peru: 1530-1780.* New York, 1932.

43. ———, "Pre-Spanish Navigation on the Andean Coast," *American Neptune,* vol. II, no. 2 (1942).

44. Monge, Carlos, *Acclimatization in the Andes,* trans. by Donald F. Brown. Baltimore, 1948.

45. Nordenskiöld, Baron Erland, *The Secret of the Peruvian Quipus.* Comparative Ethnographical Studies, no. 6. Göteborg, 1925.

46. Osborne, Harold, *Indians of the Andes: Aymaras and Quechuas*. London and Cambridge, Mass., 1952.

47. Paulsson, Gregor, *The Study of Cities*. Copenhagen, 1959.

48. Pizarro, Pedro, *Relación del Descubrimiento y Conquista de los Reinos del Perú* (written in 1570-1) in Col. Docs. ineds. Historia de España, vol. V: 201-388, Madrid, 1844.

49. ————, *Relation of the Discovery and Conquest of the Kingdoms of Perú*, trans. and ed. by P. A. Means, 2 vols. Cortez Society, New York, 1921.

50. Poma de Ayala, Felipe Guamán, *Nueva Cronica y Buen Gobierno*. Paris, 1936.

51. Posnansky, Arthur, *Tihuanacu, the Cradle of American Man*, trans. by James F. Shearer. New York, 1945-57.

52. Prescott, William H., *History of the Conquest of Peru*. New York, 1847.

53. Rowe, John H., "Inca Culture at the Time of the Spanish Conquest," in Steward (ed.), *Handbook of South American Indians*, vol. 2.

54. ————, *An Introduction to the Archaeology of Cuzco*. Papers of the Peabody Museum of American Archaeology and Ethnology, vol. XXVII, no. 2. Cambridge, Mass., 1944.

55. Salaman, Redcliffe N., *The History and Social Influence of the Potato*. Cambridge, England, 1949.

56. Sansevero, Raimondo di Saugro, *Lettera Apologetica . . .* Naples, 1750.

57. Sarmiento de Gamboa, Pedro, *History of the Incas*, trans. and ed. by Sir Clements Markham. Cambridge, England, 1907.

58. Sauer, Carl O., "Cultivated Plants of South and Central America," in Steward (ed.), *Handbook of South American Indians*, vol. 6.

59. Seton, Lloyd, "Building in Stone and Brick," in Singer, et al. (eds.) *A History of Technology*, vol. 1.

60. Shepard, Anna Osler, *Ceramics for the Archaeologist*. Carnegie Institution of Washington, Pub. 609. Washington, D. C., 1956.

61. Singer, Charles, Holonyard, E. J., and Hall, A. R. (eds.), *A History of Technology*, vols. 1, 3. New York and London, 1954, 1957.
Volume 1 of this work is a magnificent encyclopedic volume (827 pages) providing students of technology, science, and archaeology with some human and historical background for

studies of preliterate societies. A pioneer work, each part written by a specialist in its field, this volume deals mostly with the Near East and the civilizations around the Fertile Crescent. It seldom enters the American area, and when it does, it is usually wrong, e.g., the Chimú culture of Peru is dated 1200 B.C. (actually A.D. 1000) on p. 731; its information on Peru's roads is hopelessly entangled.

62. Squier, E. George, *Peru: Incidents of Travel and Exploration in the Land of the Incas.* New York, 1877.

63. Steward, Julian H. (ed.), *Handbook of South American Indians,* 6 vols. Washington, D. C., 1946-50.

64. Thompson, J. Eric S., Pollock, H. E. D., and Charlot, Jean, *A Preliminary Study of the Ruins of Cobá . . .* Carnegie Institution of Washington, Pub. 424. Washington, D. C., 1932.

65. Uhle, Max, *Las Ruinas de Tomebamba.* Quito, 1923.

66. Valcárcel, Luis E., "The Andean Calendar," in Steward (ed.), *Handbook of South American Indians,* vol. 2.

67. Violich, Francis, *Cities of Latin America.* New York, 1944.

68. Volney, Constantin, *Les Ruines: ou Méditation sur les Révolutions des Empires.* Paris, 1791.
There is an edition in English of *The Ruins* which was prepared by Count Volney himself. Although the book is rhapsodic and, as archaeology, inaccurate, still it had great influence in France, England, and the United States. It provided at this early date (1791) much stimulus toward interest in man's past.

69. Von Hagen, Victor Wolfgang, *The Four Seasons of Manuela.* New York, 1952.

70. ———, *Guide to Machu Picchu.* New York, 1945.

71. ———, *A Guide to Sacsahuaman, the Fortress of Cusco.* New York, 1949.

72. ———, *Highway of the Sun.* New York, 1955.

73. ———, "The Search for the Gilded Man," *Natural History,* vol. 61 (September, 1952), 312-21.

74. ———, *South America Called Them: Explorations of the Great Naturalists: La Condamine, Humboldt, Darwin, Spruce.* New York, 1945.

75. ———, *The Tsátchela Indians of Western Ecuador.* Indian Notes and Monographs of the Museum of the American Indian, Misc. no. 51. New York, 1939.

76. Xerez, Francisco de, *Verdadera relacion de la conquista del Peru,* Seville, 1534.
(There is an English translation by Sir Clements Markham. Pub. by the Hakluyt Society, London, 1872.)

Chronology

c. 2000 B.C. *Greeks active in Troy.*	c. 2500 B.C. Coastal Indians at Chicama engaged in agriculture.
	1200-400 B.C. Chavín de Huantar culture, central Andes.
850 B.C. *Age of Homer.*	
776 B.C. *First Olympiad held in Greece.*	
753 B.C. *Legendary founding of Rome.*	750 B.C. Costal cultures: Virú, Cupisnique, Gallinazo. Formative period in many Peruvian coastal cultures.
431-404 B.C. *Peloponnesian Wars.*	
	400 B.C.-A.D. 400 Paracas (Caverna) I. Peru, south coast on dry shores of Paracas Peninsula (Pisco).
331 B.C. *Alexander the Great defeats Darius at Arbela.*	400 B.C.-A.D. 1000 Nazca, south coastal culture.
c. 240 B.C. *Eratosthenes computes size of the earth.*	272 B.C. Carbon-14-dated appearance of Mochica culture.
	272 B.C.-A.D. 1000 Mochica coastal empire.
146 B.C. *Romans capture and destroy Carthage.*	
44 B.C. *Assassination of Julius Caesar.*	
A.D. 79 *Volcanic Destruction of Herculaneum and Pompeii.*	
c. 117 *Roman Empire at its greatest extent.*	
235 *Disintegration of Roman Empire.*	
337 *Death of Constantine.*	

Europe and North America	INCA
400-800 *The Mound Builders: Wisconsin to Gulf of Mexico.*	A.D. 400-800 Paracas (Necropolis) II.
410 *Alaric sacks Rome.*	400-1000 Tiahuanaco Empire (Andean).
500 *Pueblo Indian culture begins in Utah, Colorado, Arizona.*	
529 *Publication of the Justinian Code.*	
632 *Death of Mohammed.*	
	700 Gate of the Sun, Tiahuanaco, carved. Erected from a single piece of immense stone. The symbol of the "Weeping God" influences much of latter-day Peruvian fabric and ceramic motifs.
800 *Imperial Coronation of Charlemagne at Rome.*	800 Huari-Tiahuanaco. An offshoot of the ceremonial center about Lake Titicaca. Province of Huanta near to Ayacucho, 8,000 feet altitude.
871-899 *Alfred, king of Wessex and of England.*	
900 *Golden Age of Arabian power in Spain.*	900 Chanapata period in Cuzco. Pre-Inca occupation of valley of Cuzco.
c. 985 *Vikings settle Greenland.*	
1066-87 *William I (the conqueror), king of England.*	1000 Tiahuanaco Empire, either from regions about Titicaca or Huari, sweeps down upon the coast in religio-military conquest.
	c. 1100 Cuzco founded by legendary historical figure of Manco Capac. First Lord-Inca.
1189-92 *Third Crusade, Frederick Barbarossa, Richard the Lion-Hearted, and Philip II.*	
1227 *Death of Genghis Khan.*	
1275 *Five-year drought in American Southwest. Raid by Navaho brings end to Cliff Dweller culture.*	1250 Inca culture in and about Cuzco Valley.
	1300 Tiahuanaco coast invasion collapses. Many other cultures spring out of its ruin. Chimú, Mochic-speaking people as were the Mochicas, rise and form an immense empire; rivals of Incas.
1347 *Black Death spreads through Europe.*	1350 Incas begin expansion. Inca Roca, 6th Inca, builds bridge across the Apurimac. Quechua becomes official language.

1386 *Chaucer composes the Canterbury Tales.*	1390 Chimú, kingdom of Chimor, rules 600 miles of land, completes capital Chan-Chan.
1415 *Henry V defeats French at Agincourt.*	
	1437 Viracocha, 8th Inca. Cuzco is besieged by Chanca tribe.
1431 *Joan of Arc burned at stake.*	
	1438 Inca troops under Yupanqui, son of Viracocha, defeat Chancas. Proclaimed 9th Inca, he takes name of Pachacuti.
	1450 Chimú influence felt from Lima to Tumbes.
1450-55 *The Gutenberg Bible.*	1450 Pachacuti enlarges Inca Empire by series of local wars.
1453 *Fall of Constantinople.*	
	1463 Pachacuti directs war of extermination against Lupaca and Colla tribes centered about Lake Titicaca in the ruins of Tiahuanaco Empire.
1469 *Union of ruling houses of Castile and Aragon through marriage of Ferdinand and Isabella.*	1466 Chimú Empire is overrun by troops of Incas. Incas control all of Peru.
	1471 Topa Inca, 10th Lord-Inca. State reorganized. Era of road-building.
1483 *Richard III, last of Plantagenet kings of England, begins reign.*	1480 Inca army under Topa Inca builds roads leading into Chile, preparatory to Conquest.
	1485 Topa Inca is supposed to have marshaled a fleet of balsa rafts and sailed to the Galapágos Islands. (No scientific corroboration.)
1492 *Columbus discovers America.*	1492 Topa Inca conquers all of Chile to the Maule River. Establishes Inca fortress called Purumaucu.
1497 *North America discovered by John Cabot.*	1493 Huayna Capac, 11th Lord-Inca. Completes coastal road from Chile to Tumbes.
1498 *Columbus discovers mainland of South America.*	1498 Huayna Capac extends conquest beyond Quito into Colombia. Completes Andean highway, Quito to Talca (Chile), 3,250 miles.

1500 *Birth of Benvenuto Cellini.*	1500 Huayna Capac undertakes final conquest of Chachapoyas.
1513 *Juan Ponce de León discovers Florida.*	1513 Vasco Nuñez de Balboa discovers the Pacific. The Incas become aware of white man's presence in South America.
1519 *Magellan begins circumnavigation of the globe.*	1519 Atahualpa (age 19) destined to be last Inca, takes part in military campaigns.
	1522 Pascal de Andogoya on an expedition of small ships down toward Darien is made aware of the Kingdom of Gold (Peru).
	1525 Alejo Garcia, leading an attack of Chiriguanos on an Inca (1525) outpost in the Gran Chaco, is killed. Incas are made aware of "white men."
	1527 Francisco Pizarro makes first landing.
	1527 Death of Huayna Capac.
1529 *First siege of Vienna by the Turks.*	1527 Civil war between Huáscar, crowned 12th Inca, and Atahualpa, who dominates the north. Huáscar defeated in 1532.
	1532 (May 13) Francisco Pizarro returns to Tumbes.
	1532 (Nov. 16) Atahualpa captured by Pizarro in Cajamarca, held captive, agrees to ransom himself.
1534 *Church of England established.*	1533 (Aug. 29) His ransom completed, Atahualpa is executed for crimes against the Spaniards.
	1535 Inca Empire completely subjugated. Manco II crowned "Inca" by the Spaniards.
	1536 Manco II leads revolt, Cuzco under siege.
	1537 Siege of Cuzco lifted. Manco II retires with large force into sanctuary of Vilcapampa. Establishes Neo-Inca state.

1538 Civil war between conquistadors. Battle of Salinas. Almagro captured, executed.

1539-42 *Hernando De Soto explores the Mississippi.*

1541 Francisco Pizarro assassinated by men of Almagro.

1542 Battle of Chupas between Almagro the Younger and royal Spanish forces. Almagro defeated.

1542 "New Laws for the Indies" protects Indians; Spanish conquistadors' revolt led by Gonzalo Pizarro.

1547 *Death of Henry VIII.*

1548 La Gasca leading royal forces defeats Gonzalo Pizarro at battle of Sacsahuamán.

1551 Antonio de Mendoza named first Viceroy to Peru.

1553 Pedro de Cieza de León publishes (Seville) epoch-making *First Part of the Chronicles of Peru.*

1565 *Ivan the Terrible of Russia initiates reign of terror.*

1579 *Francis Drake explores California coast.*

1572 End of the Neo-Inca state. Tupac Amaru executed.

1588 *Defeat of Spanish Armada.*

1595 Sir Walter Raleigh explores lower part of Orinoco River in search of El Dorado.

1620 *Plymouth Colony established in Massachusetts.*

1675-76 *King Philip's War in New England.*

1601 Garcilaso de la Vega, surnamed "The Inca," born in Cuzco of a Spanish father and an Inca princess, publishes *The Royal Commentaries of the Incas.*

1680 *Pueblo revolt in Nuevo Mexico.*

1733 *Molasses Act stirs up English colonies.*

1691 Father Fritz, after years of exploration, publishes the first detailed map of the Amazon River.

1748 *Excavations at Pompeii begin.*

1767 Jesuits expelled from all the Americas by order of Charles III of Spain.

1776 *Declaration of Independence by the Thirteen Colonies.*

1780-1 Revolt of Andean Indians led by José Gabriel Condorcanqui, styled Tupac Amaru II. Tupac Amaru II is defeated and executed.

1781 End of Inca Empire.

Index